Harnessing AI

Rob May

Harnessing AI
Copyright © 2023 by Rob May

All rights reserved.
ISBN: 9798872140795

No part of this book may be reproduced in any form or by any electronic or mechanical means including information storage and retrieval systems, without permission in writing from the author. The only exception is by a reviewer, who may quote short exerts in a review.

Images are author-created using DALL-E
Cover Design by Canva

First Edition

Rob May
corporate website:
www.ramsac.com
speaking website:
www.thoughtprovoked.co.uk
X: @robmay70
LinkedIn: /in/rpvmay/

Printed in the UK

First Printing: December 2023

Dedication

To my awesome wife and children, who have been both an inspiration and an enormous support - this book wouldn't be possible without the love and joy that you bring to every aspect of my life.

To my colleagues, whose brilliant minds and collaborative spirit have not only enriched this work but have also been the cornerstone of innovation and progress within our field - your cooperation and friendship are very much appreciated.

And to the curious souls and visionary thinkers everywhere, who dare to dream of a better future and take the bold steps necessary to make it a reality, may this book serve as a compass in the fascinating odyssey of Artificial Intelligence.

Together, we stand on the brink of a new horizon. Let us step forward with courage, wisdom, and an enduring hope for what we can achieve.

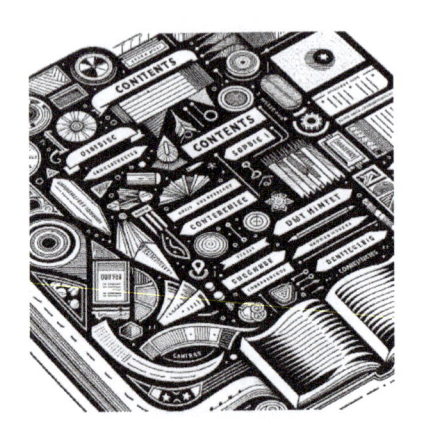

Contents

- Introduction Pg. 7
- AI in the Modern World Pg. 11
- The Foundations of AI Pg. 25
- Ethical and Legal Considerations in AI Pg. 38
- OECD Principles on AI   Pg. 67
- EU Ethics Guidelines for Trustworthy AI Pg. 70
- Building an AI Strategy Pg. 77
- How to Use AI in Your Organisation Pg. 88
- Risk Management & Contingency Plans Pg. 93
- Developing AI Capabilities Pg. 99
- Implementing AI Projects Pg. 116
- Case Studies of Successful AI Projects Pg. 123
- Ensuring Ethical and Responsible AI Implementation Pg. 127
- Measuring AI Impact and Success Pg. 134
- Quantifying AI's Business Value Pg. 147
- The Future of AI & Org. Strategy Pg. 153
- Appendices Pg. 169
- Books Pg. 176
- Websites and Online Portals Pg. 179
- Academic Journals Pg. 182

- Online Courses & Educational Platforms Pg.185
- Podcasts on AI Pg. 187
- Video Channels on AI Pg.189
- Professional Organisations & Networks Pg. 191
- AI Thought Leaders and Influencers Pg. 195
- AI Strategy Templates and Checklists Pg. 198
- AI Strategy Template – 1 Pg. 199
- AI Strategy Checklist - 2 Pg. 201
- Frequently Asked Questions about AI Pg. 206
- Conclusion Pg. 211
- The Call to Action Pg. 222
- About the Author Pg. 226

Harnessing AI

Introduction

Welcome to "Harnessing AI," a comprehensive guide designed to navigate the complex and rapidly evolving world of Artificial Intelligence (AI). This book aims to demystify AI, presenting it not as a distant, abstract concept but as a tangible and pivotal force in our modern world, reshaping industries, societies, and day-to-day lives.

The AI Revolution

AI is no longer the stuff of science fiction; it is a reality that is transforming the way we live and work. From chatbots in customer service to predictive analytics in healthcare, AI is making its presence felt across numerous domains. This book explores the exciting and sometimes daunting world of AI, offering insights into how it works, where it is headed, and how it will impact us all.

Navigating the AI Landscape

Our journey through "Harnessing AI" begins with an exploration of AI's fundamental concepts, tracing its evolution from a theoretical discipline to its current state where it stands as a cornerstone of technological advancement. We delve into the intricacies of machine learning, deep learning, and other AI technologies, elucidating how they function and are applied in various sectors.

AI in Practice

Beyond theory, this book provides a practical perspective on AI. It examines real-world applications, successes, challenges, and the transformative potential of AI in business, healthcare, education, and many other sectors. Through case studies and real-life examples, it shows how AI is not just an industrial tool but a broader societal influencer.

Ethical and Societal Implications

As AI becomes increasingly integrated into the fabric of society, its ethical and societal implications cannot be overstated. "Harnessing AI" addresses these critical issues, discussing the importance of responsible AI development, the ethical dilemmas posed, and the need for robust governance and regulatory frameworks.

Preparing for an AI-Driven Future

The book also serves as a guide for individuals and organisations preparing to navigate the AI-driven future. It offers strategies for adopting AI, enhancing AI literacy, and developing AI-ready infrastructures and policies. I provide practical advice for businesses, policymakers, educators, and professionals across various fields to adapt and thrive in this AI-augmented landscape.

A Call to Action

Finally, "Harnessing AI" culminates with a call to action, encouraging readers to engage proactively with AI. Whether you are a seasoned tech professional, a business leader, a policymaker, or simply an AI enthusiast, this book is an invitation to be part of the AI revolution – to understand it, shape it, and harness its potential for the greater good.

Welcome to "Harnessing AI." This journey will enlighten, challenge, and inspire you as we explore the remarkable world of Artificial Intelligence together. Let us embark on this journey to understand and leverage AI, preparing for a future where technology and humanity converge in unprecedented ways.

Chapter 1:
AI in the Modern World

AI and its Evolution

At the heart of modern technological advancement lies Artificial Intelligence (AI), a field that has evolved dramatically from theoretical concepts to a transformative force in virtually every sector. To understand AI's current and future impact, it is essential to look at its evolutionary journey.

The Genesis and Early Years of AI

AI's roots can be traced back to the mid-20th century when the idea of creating machines capable of intelligent behaviour first emerged. Early AI research in the 1950s and 1960s focused on developing systems that could mimic basic human problem-solving and reasoning skills. This era saw the birth of fundamental AI concepts and programming languages, such as Lisp, which played a significant role in AI development.

The Era of Symbolic AI and Rule-Based Systems

In the 1970s and 1980s, AI research shifted towards symbolic AI, which is also known as "good old-fashioned AI" (GOFAI). This approach relied on explicitly programmed rules and logic to mimic human thought processes. These rule-based systems could solve complex problems but were limited by their reliance on pre-defined rules and an inability to learn from data.

The Rise of Machine Learning and Neural Networks

The limitations of symbolic AI led to the emergence of machine learning (ML) in the late 1980s and 1990s. ML represented a paradigm shift, focusing on developing algorithms that could learn patterns and make decisions based on data. The revival of neural networks, inspired by the structure of the human brain, laid the groundwork for deep learning, a subset of machine learning that has driven significant AI breakthroughs in recent years.

The Advent of Deep Learning and Big Data

The explosion of digital data and advancements in computational power in the 21st century catalysed the rise of deep learning. These complex algorithms, powered by vast amounts of data, have enabled AI to achieve remarkable feats, from mastering complex games like Go to driving advances in natural language processing, image recognition, and autonomous vehicles.

AI Today: Integrated and Ubiquitous

Today, AI is an integral part of our daily lives, often in ways we do not realise. It powers search engines, social media algorithms, personal assistants, and more, continually learning and evolving. AI's integration into various industries has led to unprecedented efficiencies, new capabilities, and the transformation of traditional business models.

Looking Ahead: The Path Toward General AI

As AI continues to evolve, the quest for General AI (GenAI) – machines with the ability to understand, learn, and apply intelligence broadly and flexibly, like humans – remains the ultimate goal.

While GenAI remains a theoretical concept, its potential represents a profound shift in AI's evolution, promising future advancements that could redefine our interaction with technology.

Impact of AI on Various Industries

The influence of Artificial Intelligence (AI) transcends multiple sectors, revolutionising traditional practices, enhancing efficiencies, and enabling new business models. As you will see below, AI has already made significant inroads in various industries, transforming them profoundly.

Healthcare: Revolutionising Patient Care and Research

In healthcare, AI's impact is multifaceted. AI-driven diagnostic tools augment the capabilities of physicians, enabling early detection of diseases like cancer with higher accuracy. AI algorithms are also instrumental in personalising treatment plans, considering individual patient data to tailor therapies effectively. Beyond patient care, AI is accelerating drug discovery, reducing the time and cost associated with bringing new treatments to market.

Finance: Enhancing Decision-Making and Risk Management

The finance industry has embraced AI for various applications, including fraud detection, risk assessment, and algorithmic trading. AI systems analyse vast datasets to identify patterns indicative of fraudulent activities, significantly enhancing security measures. In risk management, AI provides more nuanced and dynamic risk assessments, improving decision-making processes. Algorithmic trading uses AI to execute trades at optimal times, maximising returns based on market data analysis.

Retail: Personalisation and Supply Chain Optimisation

AI is reshaping retail, primarily through personalisation and supply chain efficiencies. AI-driven recommendation engines provide personalised shopping experiences, boosting customer engagement and sales.

In supply chain management, AI optimises inventory levels and logistics, predicting demand patterns and automating restocking processes, reducing costs and improving efficiency.

Manufacturing: Driving Automation and Predictive Maintenance

In manufacturing, AI, and robotics work in tandem to automate complex tasks, increasing efficiency and reducing human error. AI-powered predictive maintenance predicts equipment failures before they occur, minimising downtime and extending machinery life. Additionally, AI assists in quality control, analysing products with high precision to ensure adherence to standards.

Agriculture: Enhancing Crop Management and Yield Prediction

AI's application in agriculture is transforming farming practices. AI-driven data analysis helps in precision farming, where inputs like water and fertilisers are optimised for efficiency and sustainability. AI models also predict crop yields, assisting farmers in planning and resource allocation, thus enhancing productivity.

Transportation: Advancing Autonomous Vehicles and Traffic Management

The transportation sector is witnessing a paradigm shift with the development of autonomous vehicles, powered by AI algorithms capable of safe and efficient navigation. AI also plays a critical role in traffic management systems, analysing traffic patterns to optimise flow and reduce congestion.

Education: Personalised Learning and Administrative Efficiency

In education, AI enables personalised learning experiences, adapting content to suit individual student needs and learning styles. AI systems also automate administrative tasks, allowing educators to focus more on teaching and student engagement.

AI's influence across these industries highlights its role as a versatile and powerful tool for innovation and improvement. Each sector benefits from AI's ability to analyse vast amounts of data, automate processes, and provide deeper insights, leading to more informed decision-making and enhanced outcomes. As AI technology continues to evolve, its potential applications and impacts across industries are bound to expand further.

Understanding General AI (GenAI) and its Potential

While AI has made remarkable strides in specific domains, the concept of General AI (GenAI) represents a frontier still largely uncharted. I think it is important to understand the concept of GenAI, its potential capabilities, and the challenges it presents.

Defining General AI

General AI refers to an advanced form of AI that can understand, learn, and apply its intelligence to a wide range of problems, much like a human being. Unlike narrow AI, which excels at specific tasks, GenAI has the potential for broad cognitive abilities, enabling it to perform any intellectual task that a human can. This concept extends beyond programmed responses or learning from large datasets to encompass reasoning, problem-solving, and creative thinking across diverse contexts.

The Potential of GenAI

The potential of GenAI is vast and transformative. It could lead to the creation of machines that can make complex decisions, solve intricate problems, and innovate in ways currently limited to human intelligence. In practical terms, GenAI could revolutionise fields such as scientific research, by hypothesising and testing new theories; creative industries, by generating innovative designs and artworks; and complex problem-solving in areas like climate change or global health crises.

Challenges and Considerations in Realising GenAI

Developing GenAI poses significant technical and ethical challenges. Technically, creating an AI system with generalised intelligence involves overcoming current limitations in machine learning, knowledge representation, and cognitive computing. It requires advancements in understanding how intelligence works, both in machines and in the human brain.

Ethically, GenAI raises profound questions. The autonomy and decision-making capabilities of GenAI systems necessitate careful consideration of ethical boundaries, responsibilities, and societal impacts. Issues such as autonomy in decision-making, safety, control, and the implications of creating machines with human-like intelligence are at the forefront of discussions surrounding GenAI.

Current State and Future Prospects of GenAI

As of now, GenAI remains a theoretical and aspirational goal. Current AI technologies, while advanced, are still far from achieving the broad, adaptable intelligence that characterises GenAI. However, research in areas like neural network architectures, cognitive science, and machine reasoning continues to push the boundaries of what might be possible. The pursuit of GenAI not only advances our technological capabilities but also deepens our understanding of human intelligence and consciousness.

The Societal Impact of GenAI

The advent of GenAI could have profound societal implications. It presents opportunities for significant advancements in various fields, but also poses challenges in terms of governance, ethical use, and the societal integration of highly intelligent AI systems. Preparing for a future where GenAI might exist involves not only technological readiness but also a robust ethical and regulatory framework.

General AI is an intriguing yet complex concept, with both its vast potential, and also the challenges it presents. GenAI represents the next frontier in AI development, offering both unprecedented opportunities and critical considerations for the future of technology and society.

The Role of AI in Shaping Tomorrow's World

Artificial Intelligence (AI) is not just a technological phenomenon; it is a catalyst for transformation, reshaping the fabric of society, business, and our daily lives. AI is poised to shape our future and we must consider the implications that this holds for various aspects of the world we inhabit.

AI as a Driver of Economic and Social Change

AI's impact on the economy is profound. It is a key driver of innovation, productivity, and economic growth. By automating routine tasks, AI enables a shift towards higher-value work, fostering new job categories and skill requirements. Beyond economics, AI has the potential to address critical social issues such as healthcare accessibility, educational advancements, and environmental conservation, contributing to broader societal benefits.

Transforming Industries and Workplaces

AI is revolutionising industries by enabling new business models and disrupting existing ones. In the workplace, AI's role extends from being a tool for efficiency to a collaborator enhancing human capabilities. The nature of work is evolving, with AI taking on repetitive tasks and humans focusing on complex problem-solving, strategic planning, and creative endeavours. This shift necessitates a rethinking of job roles, organisational structures, and employee training.

Ethical and Governance Challenges

As AI becomes more integrated into our lives, it brings ethical and governance challenges that need addressing. Issues like privacy, surveillance, bias in AI algorithms, and the potential for job displacement require careful consideration and management. Establishing robust ethical frameworks and governance structures is crucial to ensure AI's benefits are distributed equitably and responsibly.

AI in Personal Lives and Society

On a personal level, AI is influencing lifestyle, behaviour, and social interactions. From smart home devices to AI-enabled healthcare, AI technology is becoming an integral part of daily life. This integration raises questions about dependency on technology, data privacy, and the nature of human-AI interaction. Society needs to navigate these changes, balancing the benefits of AI with maintaining personal autonomy and social values.

Preparing for an AI-Driven Future

Looking forward, preparing for an AI-driven future is essential for individuals, businesses, and governments. This includes fostering AI literacy, adapting educational systems to focus on skills complementary to AI, and developing policies that support a sustainable and equitable AI ecosystem.

Embracing AI's potential while mitigating its risks will be key to harnessing its power for a better future.

A Balanced Approach to AI Adoption

AI's role in shaping tomorrow's world is undeniable. It presents us with opportunities for significant advancements but also challenges that require thoughtful consideration. A balanced approach to AI adoption, emphasising ethical use, inclusivity, and sustainable development, will be crucial.

As we stand on the cusp of this AI era, our collective actions and decisions will shape the impact AI has on our world.

As you can see AI will have a profound influence on the future when we consider its economic, social, ethical, and personal impacts. This book aims to provide a balanced view of the opportunities and challenges AI presents, urging a thoughtful and responsible approach to its integration into our world.

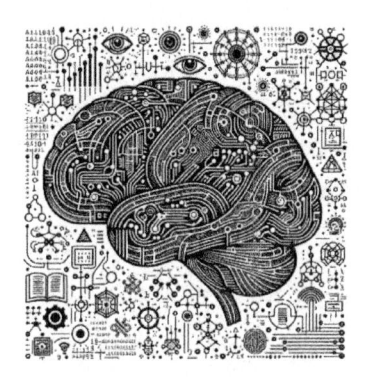

Chapter 2:
The Foundations of AI

Key Concepts and Technologies in AI

To fully grasp the potential of Artificial Intelligence (AI) and its implications, it is crucial to understand the foundational concepts and technologies that underpin it. Here we explore these fundamental elements, providing a clear overview of the building blocks of AI.

Understanding the Basics of AI

AI, at its core, involves creating machines capable of performing tasks that typically require human intelligence. This includes abilities like learning, reasoning, problem-solving, perception, and language understanding. The development of AI systems involves various disciplines, including computer science, cognitive science, linguistics, psychology, and much more, reflecting the complex interdisciplinary nature of the field.

Machine Learning: The Engine of AI

Machine Learning (ML) is a subset of AI where machines learn from data. Unlike traditional programming, where rules are explicitly coded, ML algorithms learn patterns and make decisions with minimal human intervention. ML is categorised into three main types: supervised learning, where the algorithm learns from labelled data; unsupervised learning, where it identifies patterns in unlabelled data; and reinforcement learning, where it learns through trial and error to achieve a specific goal.

Deep Learning: A Leap Forward

Deep Learning, a further subset of ML, involves neural networks with multiple layers (hence 'deep') that process data in complex ways. Inspired by the human brain's structure, deep learning has been crucial in advancing AI capabilities, particularly in processing unstructured data like images and speech. It is the technology behind many contemporary AI breakthroughs, including facial recognition and natural language processing.

Natural Language Processing (NLP) and Computer Vision

NLP is a field of AI focused on enabling machines to understand and interact with human language. This technology powers chatbots, translation services, and voice assistants. Computer vision, on the other hand, enables machines to interpret and make decisions based on visual data, akin to human sight. Applications range from image and video analysis to autonomous vehicles.

Emerging Technologies: Quantum AI and Edge AI

As AI evolves, innovative technologies emerge. Quantum AI, which combines quantum computing with AI, promises to process complex problems at unprecedented speeds.

Edge AI refers to AI algorithms processed locally on devices like smartphones or IoT devices, reducing the need for data transmission to centralised servers. These emerging technologies indicate the dynamic and ever-evolving nature of AI.

Machine Learning, Deep Learning, and Beyond

Now we need to delve deeper into the realms of Machine Learning (ML), Deep Learning (DL), and the cutting-edge advancements that are shaping the future of AI.

Machine Learning: Beyond Traditional Programming

Machine Learning represents a transformation in how we approach problem-solving in computing. Unlike traditional programming that relies on explicit instructions, machine learning uses algorithms that learn from data. This ability to learn and adapt makes ML a powerful tool in AI's arsenal.

There are three primary types of ML as follows:

1. **Supervised Learning:** Here, the algorithm learns from a labelled dataset, making predictions or decisions based on that training. It is widely used in applications like spam detection and credit scoring.

2. **Unsupervised Learning:** This involves learning from data that is not labelled and finding hidden patterns or intrinsic structures in the data. It is useful in clustering and

association tasks, like customer segmentation in marketing.

3. **Reinforcement Learning:** In this approach, an algorithm learns to make decisions by performing actions and receiving feedback from those actions, akin to learning through trial and error. It is instrumental in areas like robotics and gaming.

Deep Learning: Mimicking the Human Brain

Deep Learning, a subset of machine learning, is inspired by the structure and function of the human brain, specifically neural networks. DL uses multi-layered neural networks to analyse various factors of data, allowing it to handle complex tasks like image and speech recognition with remarkable accuracy. The layers in deep learning models are capable of learning features and patterns at multiple levels of abstraction, making it highly effective for complex, large-scale AI applications.

Breakthroughs in Deep Learning

The advancements in deep learning have led to significant breakthroughs:

Image and Video Recognition: DL models excel at analysing and interpreting visual content, leading to advances in facial recognition, medical imaging, and autonomous vehicles.

Natural Language Processing (NLP): Deep learning has transformed NLP, enabling more natural and effective human-computer interactions. This is evident in chatbots, translation services, and voice recognition systems.

Generative Models: Techniques like Generative Adversarial Networks (GANs) are creating new possibilities in content creation, ranging from art and music to synthetic data generation.

Emerging Trends and Future Directions

As AI continues to advance, new trends and technologies are emerging:

Explainable AI (XAI): As AI systems become more complex, there is a growing need for transparency. XAI aims to make AI decision-making processes clear and understandable to humans.

AI in Edge Computing: Edge AI involves processing AI algorithms on local devices (like smartphones or IoT devices), reducing latency and bandwidth use.

Quantum Machine Learning: Combining quantum computing with ML, this field promises to solve complex problems more efficiently than classical computers.

These critical aspects of machine learning, deep learning, and their evolving frontiers form the backbone of AI's capabilities and are central to its current and future applications.

The Role of Data in AI

Data is the lifeblood of Artificial Intelligence (AI). As we explore the critical role of data in AI, it is important to also consider the challenges surrounding it, and the ethical considerations in its use.

Data: The Foundation of AI Systems

AI systems, particularly those based on machine learning and deep learning, rely heavily on data for training and operation. The quality, quantity, and variety of data directly impact the performance and accuracy of AI models. Data is used to train AI systems, allowing them to learn, adapt, and make predictions or decisions. This makes the collection and processing of high-quality data a fundamental step in AI development.

Challenges in Data Collection and Processing

Collecting and processing data for AI presents several challenges:

Volume and Variety: AI systems require large volumes of diverse data to perform well. Gathering and processing this data can be resource intensive.

Quality and Bias: The quality of data is crucial. Poor quality or biased data can lead to inaccurate or unfair AI decisions. Ensuring data accuracy and removing biases is a significant challenge in AI development.

Data Privacy and Security: With the increasing use of personal data, maintaining privacy and security is paramount. AI developers must navigate complex data protection regulations and ethical considerations.

Big Data and AI

The advent of big data has been a boon for AI. Big data refers to extremely large datasets that can be analysed computationally to reveal patterns, trends, and associations. The relationship between big data and AI is symbiotic: while AI enables the extraction of insights from big data, big data feeds AI with the information necessary for learning and evolution.

Ethical Considerations in AI Data Use

The use of data in AI raises several ethical concerns:

Privacy: As AI systems often use personal data, protecting individual privacy is a major concern. Adhering to privacy laws and ensuring informed consent for data use are crucial.

Bias and Fairness: AI systems can perpetuate and amplify biases present in the training data. Ensuring fairness in AI involves careful data curation and the development of algorithms that can identify and mitigate biases.

Transparency and Accountability: The sources of data and the methods of its use in AI should be transparent. It is essential to establish clear accountability for data-related decisions in AI systems.

Towards Responsible Data Use in AI

For AI to be effective and ethical, responsible data use is essential. This involves implementing robust data governance practices, ensuring data quality, and addressing privacy and ethical concerns from the outset. Balancing the pursuit of advanced AI capabilities with responsible data practices is key to the sustainable and ethical development of AI technologies.

Data has a pivotal role in AI, but it also presents many challenges, and the ethical dimensions in its use cannot be ignored. Understanding and addressing these aspects is crucial for the development of effective and responsible AI systems both in our organisations and in society as a whole.

Emerging Technologies and Innovations in AI

AI is a dynamic and rapidly evolving field, with new technologies and innovations continuously emerging. These are some of the cutting-edge developments shaping the future of AI.

Advancements in Machine Learning Algorithms

Recent years have seen significant advancements in machine learning algorithms. These include:

Federated Learning: An approach where AI models are trained across multiple decentralised devices or servers holding local data samples, without exchanging them. This method enhances privacy and reduces data centralisation.

Transfer Learning: This technique involves pre-training a model on one task and fine-tuning it for a different but related task. It is efficient in terms of data and computation and is widely used in NLP and computer vision.

Neuro-Symbolic AI: Combining neural networks with symbolic AI, this approach aims to create more versatile and interpretable AI systems. It seeks to blend learning from data with rule-based reasoning.

Quantum Computing and AI

Quantum computing promises to revolutionise AI by offering unprecedented processing power. Quantum AI could solve complex optimisation problems faster than classical computers and enhance the capabilities of machine learning models. While still in the emerging stage, quantum AI has the potential to significantly accelerate AI research and applications.

AI in Edge Computing

Edge AI refers to AI algorithms processed on local devices like smartphones, IoT devices, or edge servers. This approach reduces latency, conserves bandwidth, and improves data privacy. Edge AI is becoming increasingly important in applications like autonomous vehicles, smart cities, and real-time data analytics.

Explainable AI (XAI)

As AI systems become more complex, the need for transparency and understandability increases. Explainable AI aims to make AI decision-making processes more transparent, allowing humans to understand, trust, and manage AI solutions effectively. XAI is particularly important in critical applications like healthcare and finance, where understanding AI decisions is essential.

AI for Social Good

AI is being increasingly leveraged to address social and environmental challenges. From combating climate change to improving healthcare and education, AI for social good focuses on applying AI technologies to create positive societal impact. This includes using AI to analyse climate patterns, diagnose diseases more accurately, and personalise education.

AI Governance and Ethics

As AI becomes more embedded in our lives, the importance of governance and ethical frameworks grows. This involves developing standards and policies to guide the ethical development and use of AI. Key areas include ensuring AI fairness, accountability, privacy, and safety.

This is the exciting and ever-changing landscape of AI technologies and innovations. These emerging areas not only push the boundaries of what AI can achieve but also bring new considerations in terms of ethics, governance, and societal impact.

Chapter 3:
Ethical and Legal Considerations in AI

Navigating the Ethical Implications of AI

The rapid advancement of AI technology has ushered in a plethora of ethical considerations. Now I want to delve into the primary ethical dilemmas posed by AI and propose approaches to navigate these complex issues.

Bias and Fairness

One of the most pressing ethical concerns in AI is the risk of algorithmic bias, where AI systems may exhibit prejudiced behaviours based on their training data. This can lead to unfair outcomes in various applications, from job recruitment to loan approvals.

Identifying and Mitigating Bias in AI systems is a critical challenge that stands at the forefront of ethical AI development. Biases in training data and algorithms can lead to unfair, and sometimes harmful, outcomes when AI systems are deployed in real-world scenarios. To address this, a multifaceted approach is necessary—one that combines technical rigour with an awareness of the broader societal context in which AI operates. Strategies for identifying bias often begin with a thorough examination of the training data. This involves assessing the data for representativeness and diversity, ensuring that it accurately reflects the varied demographics and scenarios the AI will encounter. Techniques such as disparity analysis can uncover imbalances or skewed distributions that might predispose an algorithm towards biased decisions.

Once potential data biases are identified, the focus shifts on to the algorithms themselves. Algorithmic auditing is a technique that scrutinises AI models for biases and unfair decision patterns. Audits can be performed internally by teams of data scientists and ethicists or by independent external bodies for a more objective evaluation. Regular and rigorous audits, combined with transparency in AI processes, can help in detecting biases that may have been inadvertently encoded into AI systems. Mitigation techniques involve not just rectifying the input data, but also refining the algorithmic models.

Rebalancing or augmenting data sets, applying fairness constraints during model training, and employing interpretable machine learning models are some ways to reduce bias. Additionally, involving a diverse team in the AI development process can provide multiple perspectives that help in recognising and addressing subtle biases.

Ultimately, combating bias in AI is an ongoing process that benefits from continuous monitoring and feedback loops. As AI systems learn and evolve, new biases may emerge, necessitating vigilance and adaptability in mitigation strategies. The goal is to create AI that operates fairly and equitably, fostering trust and delivering consistent value across all user demographics and applications.

Diverse Data and Teams: The emphasis on using diverse datasets and involving multidisciplinary teams in AI development is pivotal in reducing bias and ensuring that AI systems are fair and effective for a wide range of users. Diverse datasets are fundamental to the training of AI models; they ensure that the AI systems are exposed to a wide spectrum of perspectives, scenarios, and variables. When datasets are limited or skewed towards certain demographics, behaviours, or conditions, AI models can develop biases, leading to unfair or inaccurate outcomes. Incorporating a variety of data sources that reflect different genders, ethnicities, ages, geographies, and socio-economic backgrounds can help create more balanced and inclusive AI systems. This diversity in data helps AI models to better understand and serve the needs of diverse populations, leading to more equitable and effective solutions.

In addition to diverse datasets, the involvement of multidisciplinary teams in AI development is crucial. AI is not just a technical field; it intersects with social, ethical, and cultural aspects of human life. By involving professionals from various disciplines such as social sciences, humanities, ethics, law, and design, along with technical experts, AI development can benefit from a broader range of insights and considerations. This diversity in team composition ensures that different viewpoints are considered during the development process, leading to the identification and mitigation of potential biases. Multidisciplinary teams can also better anticipate how AI systems might interact with different aspects of society and culture, leading to more responsible and context-aware AI solutions.

Overall, leveraging diverse datasets and multidisciplinary teams in AI development is not merely a best practice; it's a necessity for creating AI systems that are equitable, unbiased, and truly beneficial across different segments of society. This approach fosters the creation of AI technologies that are not only technically proficient but also socially and ethically sound.

Privacy and Surveillance
AI's ability to process vast amounts of data raises significant privacy concerns. The potential for mass surveillance using AI technologies poses ethical dilemmas regarding individual rights and freedoms.

Data Privacy Laws: Adhering to data privacy laws and regulations is fundamental in AI development. It ensures compliance with legal standards, aligns with ethical practices, builds public trust, prevents misuse, and fosters responsible innovation. As AI continues to evolve, its developers must navigate the complex landscape of data privacy with a commitment to uphold these essential principles.

Ethical Data Use: Key aspects of ethical data use include obtaining informed consent from data subjects, ensuring transparency about how and why data is being used, and implementing measures to protect data privacy and security. This involves anonymising personal data where possible, safeguarding against unauthorised access, and ensuring data is used only for its intended purpose. Ethical data use also requires regular audits and compliance checks to ensure ongoing adherence to ethical standards and legal requirements. By prioritising ethical data practices, AI developers can build trust, foster responsible innovation, and create AI systems that are both beneficial and respectful of individual rights.

AI Autonomy

As AI systems become more autonomous, questions about decision-making processes and their implications in critical areas emerge. This includes considerations in sectors like healthcare, law enforcement, and military applications.

Limits of AI Autonomy: Setting clear boundaries for AI decision-making autonomy, particularly in high-stakes scenarios.

Human Oversight: Advocating for continuous human oversight in AI systems to ensure ethical and responsible decision-making.

Accountability

Determining accountability in AI-driven decisions, especially when they lead to unintended or harmful outcomes, is a complex ethical challenge.

Transparent Decision-Making: The push for this in AI development centres on creating systems whose operations and rationale can be understood by users and stakeholders. This transparency is crucial for building trust, facilitating accountability, and ensuring fairness in AI applications. Transparent AI systems allow for an audit trail of decisions made, offering clarity on how and why specific outcomes are reached. This is particularly important in sectors where AI's decisions have significant consequences, such as healthcare, finance, and law.

Encouraging transparency also involves developing AI models that are interpretable, where the logic behind their decision-making processes can be easily communicated and understood. This not only aids in identifying and correcting biases but also fosters user confidence and acceptance. Overall, transparent AI decision-making supports ethical AI practices, compliance with regulatory standards, and the development of AI technologies that are more aligned with societal values and norms.

Legal and Moral Responsibility: This issue in cases of AI errors or malfunctions is a complex and evolving area. Generally, responsibility is attributed to the developers and deployers of AI systems, rather than the AI itself or its end-users. Developers bear the responsibility for ensuring that AI systems are designed with safety, reliability, and ethical considerations in mind. This includes thorough testing, risk assessments, and incorporating mechanisms to identify and rectify biases or potential harms. Deployers or organisations that implement AI systems in real-world settings also share in this responsibility. They must ensure proper use, monitor performance, and maintain systems to prevent malfunctions. The AI itself, lacking legal personhood or consciousness, is not held responsible. End-users, typically, are not responsible unless they misuse the AI in ways that deviate from its intended purpose. As AI technology and its societal implications continue to evolve, there is an ongoing debate about creating more nuanced legal frameworks to address these issues, ensuring that responsibility and accountability are clearly defined and fairly distributed.

Ethical AI Development

Promoting an ethical approach to AI development involves a commitment to these principles at all stages of AI design, development, and deployment.

Ethical Guidelines and Standards: In AI development these are essential to ensure that AI systems are created and used in ways that are beneficial, fair, and respect human rights. These guidelines often emphasise principles such as transparency, accountability, fairness, and respect for user privacy and autonomy. They advocate for the involvement of diverse stakeholders in the development process to ensure that diverse perspectives are considered, thereby reducing biases and increasing the inclusivity of AI systems. Best practices also include rigorous testing and validation of AI systems to ensure they are safe and reliable, and continuous monitoring post-deployment to identify and address any unintended consequences. Ethical AI development also involves adhering to existing laws and regulations and staying informed about emerging ethical concerns and societal expectations. These guidelines and standards serve not just as a moral compass but also as a framework for sustainable and trustworthy AI innovation.

Stakeholder Engagement: Involving diverse stakeholders, including ethicists, sociologists, and the public, in the development of AI to ensure a broad range of perspectives is considered.

These are the key ethical challenges presented by AI along with guidance on how to address them responsibly. Navigating these ethical implications is crucial for the sustainable and beneficial development of AI technologies.

Understanding AI and Data Privacy Laws

The integration of AI into various sectors brings it under the horizon of numerous data privacy laws and regulations. In the following pages, I've shown the intricate relationship between AI and data privacy, highlighting key legal frameworks and their implications for AI development and deployment.

The Landscape of Data Protection Regulations

AI systems often process substantial amounts of personal data, making compliance with data protection regulations a top priority. Here is an overview of the major data protection laws:

General Data Protection Regulation (GDPR): The GDPR in the European Union, and its equivalent UK GDPR, sets out stringent rules for data processing and grants individuals' significant control over their data.

Other Global Data Protection Laws: Other major data privacy regulations worldwide, such as the California Consumer Privacy Act (CCPA) in the

United States and the Personal Data Protection Act (PDPA) in Singapore should also be considered.

AI and Data Privacy Challenges

The use of personal data in AI poses unique challenges. Key considerations include:

Consent and Transparency: The principles of consent and transparency are crucial in AI, particularly when it concerning data use. Obtaining explicit consent for data use involves clearly informing individuals about what data is being collected, how it will be used, and for what purposes, ensuring that individuals have a clear and informed choice in the matter. This respect for user autonomy is a cornerstone of ethical data practices and is often mandated by data protection regulations. However, ensuring transparency in AI systems presents challenges, especially with complex algorithms where decision-making processes are not easily interpretable. The 'black box' nature of some AI models makes it difficult for users and even developers to understand exactly how inputs are being processed into outputs. Addressing these challenges requires efforts towards developing more interpretable AI models, as well as providing clear and understandable explanations to users about how their data is being used. Efforts in this direction not only fulfil ethical and legal obligations but also build trust and confidence among users, which is essential for the wider acceptance and success of AI technologies.

Data Minimisation and Purpose Limitation: These are key principles in the context of AI, particularly when balancing the need for extensive datasets with privacy concerns. Data minimisation refers to the practice of collecting only the data that is directly necessary and relevant for the specified purpose. This approach helps to protect individual privacy by reducing the likelihood of unnecessary or excessive data collection. Purpose limitation complements this by ensuring that data is used only for the specific purposes for which it was collected, and not repurposed in ways that the data subjects did not consent to. These principles are critical in AI development, where large datasets are often required for training and improving algorithms. Implementing data minimisation and purpose limitation in AI involves careful planning and clear definition of objectives at the outset of any data collection or AI project. This ensures that the collected data aligns closely with the intended goals, without overstepping into areas that infringe on personal privacy. Adhering to these principles helps balance the need for data to develop effective AI systems with the ethical imperative to respect and protect individual privacy.

Intellectual Property Rights in AI

We also need to touch on the intellectual property (IP) considerations in AI:

Ownership of AI-Generated Content: The question of ownership of AI-generated content, including artwork, text, or code, is an emerging and complex legal issue. Currently, there is no universal consensus or established legal framework that clearly defines who owns content created by AI systems. Traditional intellectual property laws are centred around human creators, leaving a grey area when it comes to content generated autonomously by AI. Various arguments exist, some propose that the creators or owners of the AI system should own the generated content, considering the investment in and development of the AI technology. Others argue for treating AI as a 'tool' used by human operators, thus attributing ownership to the individual or entity that directed the AI's output. There are also discussions around the possibility of granting AI some form of legal status in terms of content creation, though this is a more radical and less widely accepted view. The resolution of these issues will require legal evolution and potentially new legislation that specifically addresses the nuances of AI and its creative capabilities. This summary highlights the need for legal systems to adapt to technological advancements and find a balance that respects traditional IP rights while acknowledging the unique nature of AI-generated content.

Patenting AI Inventions: Patenting AI inventions and algorithms presents complex challenges within the current legal frameworks, which were primarily designed for human inventors and traditional inventions. The central issue revolves around whether AI systems can be recognised as inventors in patent law, a concept that traditional patent systems are not readily equipped to handle.

Currently, most legal systems require a human inventor for patent applications, leaving AI-generated inventions in a grey 2area. Additionally, the process of AI development, often involving machine learning and adaptive algorithms, complicates the clear definition of what exactly constitutes the 'invention' in AI systems.

There have been cases where attempts to list AI as an inventor were rejected by patent offices, reinforcing the stance that inventors must be human beings. However, this raises questions about the ownership and recognition of innovations that are primarily developed by AI, without direct human input in the creative process.

Moreover, the rapid pace of AI development and its iterative nature also pose challenges in meeting traditional patent criteria like novelty and non-obviousness. As AI technologies evolve, so too does the need for legal systems to adapt and possibly rethink the criteria and definitions regarding inventorship, ownership, and patentability in the context of AI. This ongoing debate is critical for incentivising innovation in the AI field while ensuring fair recognition and protection of intellectual property.

Liability and AI

As AI systems become more autonomous, determining liability in cases where AI causes harm is increasingly important. This includes:

Liability Frameworks: Existing legal frameworks for liability, including product liability, negligence, and strict liability, face challenges when applied to AI due to the unique nature of these systems. In traditional scenarios, liability is typically clear-cut and attributed to human actors or organisations. However, AI complicates this due to its autonomous decision-making capabilities and the potential lack of human oversight in certain scenarios.

In the context of product liability, AI systems as products could hold manufacturers or developers liable if the AI causes harm due to defects or failures. This is straightforward in cases where the harm results from issues like programming errors or hardware malfunctions. However, it becomes more complex with AI systems that learn and evolve over time, where it might be difficult to pinpoint a defect or establish a standard of 'reasonable safety'.

Negligence liability involves assessing whether due care was taken in the development and deployment of the AI. This includes considering if reasonable steps were taken to prevent foreseeable harm. For AI, this could involve adequate testing, risk assessments, and ensuring transparency in AI decision-making processes.

Strict liability, which holds creators or owners liable for harm regardless of fault or negligence, poses significant challenges with AI. It raises questions about who is considered the 'owner' or 'creator' of an AI system, especially when multiple parties are involved in its development, deployment, and maintenance.

Overall, these liability frameworks need adaptation and clarification to effectively address the intricacies of AI. This includes considering the level of autonomy of the AI system, the foreseeability of harm, the role of human oversight, and the distribution of responsibilities among all parties involved in the AI lifecycle. As AI continues to advance, there is a growing need for legal frameworks to evolve in parallel, ensuring appropriate and fair attribution of liability.

Legal Reforms and AI: The rapid advancement and unique characteristics of Artificial Intelligence (AI) necessitate significant legal reforms to address challenges that traditional legal frameworks are not equipped to handle. Current laws often fail to adequately address the complexities and novel scenarios presented by AI, such as determining liability for autonomous decisions or the legal status of AI as inventors or creators. This gap underscores the need for legal reforms that can accommodate the evolving landscape of AI technology.

One major area of reform is the consideration of creating new legal categories specifically for AI systems. This could involve recognising AI as a new legal entity or developing a separate set of rules and standards that apply uniquely to AI, particularly in areas like liability, intellectual property, and rights. Such reforms would aim to provide clearer guidelines on how AI is to be treated under the law, taking into account its autonomy, learning capabilities, and interaction with humans and other systems.

Additionally, reforms are needed to update existing laws in areas such as privacy, data protection, consumer rights, and employment to reflect the realities of an AI-driven world. These updates would address issues like data usage by AI, the impact of AI on the workforce, and the rights of individuals interacting with AI systems.

The implementation of legal reforms in response to AI also involves balancing the need to regulate and control AI technology with the need to encourage innovation and development in the field. This delicate balance requires a nuanced approach that involves stakeholders from various sectors, including legal experts, technologists, ethicists, and policymakers.

The emergence of AI as a transformative technology poses unique legal challenges that require thoughtful and forward-looking legal reforms. These reforms should aim to create frameworks that ensure responsible development and use of AI while fostering innovation and protecting the rights and interests of individuals and society as a whole.

Development of Specific AI Legislation

AI-Specific Laws and Regulations: Given the unique characteristics and capabilities of Artificial Intelligence (AI), there is a growing consensus among legal experts on the need for AI-specific laws and regulations. Traditional legal frameworks often fall short in addressing the novel issues posed by AI, leading to calls for tailored legislation that can adequately govern AI's distinct attributes. Anticipated AI-specific laws are expected to cover several key areas:

AI Autonomy: Laws may be developed to address the level of autonomy AI systems possess, defining legal boundaries and responsibilities associated with autonomous decision-making. This includes determining the extent to which AI can make decisions without human intervention and the legal implications of those decisions.

Decision-Making Processes: Given the complexity and often opaque nature of AI algorithms, new regulations may focus on ensuring transparency and accountability in AI's decision-making processes. This could involve requirements for explainability, where AI systems must be able to provide understandable justifications for their decisions.

Ethical Implications: AI-specific laws are likely to address the broader ethical implications of AI systems. This includes ensuring that AI operates within ethical boundaries, respects human rights, and does not perpetuate biases or discrimination.

Data Use and Privacy: Given AI's reliance on large datasets, AI-specific laws may include stringent rules on data collection, usage, and privacy, ensuring that AI respects individual privacy rights and data protection standards.

Safety and Liability: New laws may be introduced to ensure the safety and reliability of AI systems, including provisions for liability in cases of malfunctions or accidents involving AI.

Intellectual Property: As AI systems increasingly become involved in creative and inventive processes, AI-specific legislation may redefine aspects of intellectual property law, particularly regarding AI-generated content and inventions.

The development of AI-specific laws and regulations represents an essential step in the responsible management of AI technology. By addressing issues unique to AI, such legislation aims to harness the benefits of AI while mitigating potential risks and ethical concerns, ensuring that AI development aligns with societal values and legal norms.

Global Standards and Norms: There is a growing call for international standards to govern AI. This could lead to the establishment of universal norms and guidelines that help harmonise AI regulations across different jurisdictions.

Clarifying Liability and Responsibility

Liability in AI-induced Incidents: One of the critical areas of legal evolution will be clarifying liability for damages or harm caused by AI decisions or actions. This might involve revisiting and revising current liability frameworks to accommodate the autonomous nature of AI systems.

Accountability Frameworks: Future legal trends may include developing clearer frameworks for accountability in AI, particularly in cases where decision-making is opaque or fully automated. These frameworks could determine responsibility among AI developers, users, and even the AI system itself.

Privacy Laws Tailored to AI

Enhanced Data Protection: As AI systems require vast amounts of data, including personal data, we may see more stringent privacy regulations specifically tailored to AI. These laws could address consent mechanisms, data minimisation standards, and individuals' rights over their data used in AI systems.

Anonymisation Techniques: Legal trends might also focus on promoting and mandating advanced data anonymisation techniques in AI to protect individual privacy, especially in sensitive sectors like healthcare and finance.

Intellectual Property Rights Adaptation

AI and Copyright: As AI becomes more capable of creating original content, we might see legal debates and subsequent regulations around copyright for AI-generated works, including questions of authorship and ownership.

Patent Laws and AI: The trend could also involve adapting patent laws to cater to AI innovations, potentially considering AI as an inventor or addressing the patentability of AI-generated inventions.

Ethical Governance and AI

Incorporating Ethics into Law: The trend towards incorporating ethics into law for AI regulation is a response to the growing recognition that legal compliance alone is not sufficient for the responsible development and deployment of AI systems. This anticipates a shift in regulatory approaches that integrates ethical considerations into legal frameworks, ensuring that AI technologies align with societal values and ethical norms. Such an approach acknowledges that AI, due to its far-reaching impact, requires governance that goes beyond technical legality and addresses broader moral concerns.

The embedding of ethics into AI regulations would involve setting standards that prioritise human dignity, fairness, accountability, and transparency. This means that AI systems would need to be designed and operated in ways that respect human rights, avoid bias and discrimination, and are accountable for their actions and decisions. In practice, this could involve mandatory ethical impact assessments for new AI technologies, much like environmental impact assessments in other industries.

Moreover, embedding ethics into law would require a collaborative effort from the policymakers, technologists, ethicists, and various stakeholders, ensuring a multidisciplinary approach to AI governance. This would help in translating abstract ethical principles into concrete legal requirements that are applicable and enforceable in real-world AI applications.

Regulatory Bodies for AI Ethics: The establishment of dedicated regulatory bodies or committees to oversee the ethical deployment of AI could become a norm, offering guidance and monitoring compliance with ethical standards.

These anticipated legal trends indicate a dynamic and responsive legal system adapting to the rapid advancements in AI. As AI continues to push the boundaries of technology, the legal system will play a crucial role in ensuring that this growth is balanced with societal norms, ethical considerations, and individual rights.

The Importance of International Cooperation in AI Legal Frameworks

In the realm of Artificial Intelligence (AI), the necessity for international cooperation in establishing legal frameworks is paramount. I believe that global collaboration is crucial for the development of cohesive and effective AI laws and regulations.

Harmonising AI Regulations Across Borders

Avoiding Regulatory Fragmentation: With AI technologies operating globally, disparate legal frameworks across different countries can lead to regulatory fragmentation. International cooperation helps in harmonising these regulations, ensuring consistency and predictability for global AI initiatives.

Facilitating International Trade and Innovation: A unified approach to AI regulation can facilitate international trade and AI-driven innovation, allowing companies to operate across borders without navigating a complex web of differing regulations.

Addressing Global Ethical and Societal Concerns

Consensus on Ethical Standards: AI's impact transcends national boundaries, raising ethical issues of global concern. International cooperation is vital in reaching a consensus on ethical standards for AI, ensuring that AI development aligns with shared human values and rights.

Global Response to Societal Challenges: AI has the potential to address global challenges like climate change, health crises, and inequality. Coordinated legal frameworks can foster international collaborations in AI research and applications, maximising AI's benefits for global societal good.

Learning from Diverse Perspectives

Incorporating a Range of Viewpoints: International cooperation brings diverse perspectives to the table, which is essential in developing legal frameworks that are inclusive and sensitive to different cultural, social, and economic contexts.

Sharing Best Practices and Lessons Learned: Countries at different stages of AI adoption can learn from each other's experiences. International forums and collaborations provide platforms for sharing best practices, insights, and lessons learned in AI regulation.

Developing Standards for Emerging Technologies

Staying Ahead of Rapid Technological Advancements: AI technology is advancing rapidly, often outpacing national legal systems. International cooperation can help in developing agile and forward-looking legal frameworks that can adapt to emerging AI technologies.

Setting Global Standards for New AI Applications: As new applications of AI emerge, such as autonomous weapons or advanced surveillance technologies, international cooperation becomes crucial in setting global standards and norms to govern their use.

Challenges and Opportunities in International Cooperation

Balancing National Interests with Global Goals: One of the main challenges in international cooperation is balancing national interests and sovereignty with global goals for AI. Finding common ground requires diplomacy, negotiation, and a willingness to compromise.

Opportunities for Global Leadership: There is an opportunity for international bodies and leading nations to take the initiative in fostering global cooperation in AI. This could involve creating international AI governance bodies or treaties similar to those in other fields like climate change or nuclear non-proliferation.

International cooperation in developing AI legal frameworks is not just beneficial but essential in ensuring that AI grows in a way that is ethical, responsible, and beneficial for all. This approach fosters a global AI ecosystem that respects individual rights, promotes innovation, and addresses shared challenges.

Ensuring Fairness and Transparency in AI Systems

As Artificial Intelligence (AI) systems increasingly influence various aspects of society, ensuring their fairness and transparency becomes imperative. There are strategies and practices to enhance the ethical integrity of AI systems.

Strategies for Fair AI

Fairness in AI is about ensuring that AI systems do not perpetuate or exacerbate biases and inequalities. Key strategies include:

Diverse and Representative Data: Using datasets that are diverse and representative of the entire population is a critical strategy in reducing biases in AI outcomes. AI systems learn and make decisions based on the data they are trained on. If this data is skewed or lacks diversity, the AI is likely to develop biases, leading to unfair or inaccurate outcomes. For instance, an AI system trained predominantly on data from one demographic group may perform poorly for individuals outside of that group or even perpetuate existing stereotypes and inequalities.

Diverse and representative datasets encompass a wide range of characteristics such as age, gender, ethnicity, socioeconomic status, and more, ensuring that the AI system's training data reflects the variety found in the real world. This inclusivity in data helps AI systems to better understand and serve the needs of diverse populations, leading to more equitable and effective outcomes.

Incorporating diversity in data is not only a technical requirement but also an ethical imperative. It demonstrates a commitment to fairness and equality in AI applications. As AI becomes more integrated into critical areas like healthcare, law enforcement, and financial services, the importance of using diverse and representative data becomes even more pronounced. By prioritising this approach, developers can create AI systems that are not only technically proficient but also socially responsible and fair.

Algorithmic Auditing: Regularly auditing AI algorithms for biases and discriminatory patterns is crucial. Independent audits can provide an objective assessment of AI fairness.

Inclusive Design and Development: Involving a diverse group of people in AI design and development, including those from underrepresented groups, can provide varied perspectives and help identify potential issues of fairness.

Transparency in AI

Transparency in AI refers to the ability to understand and trace how AI systems make decisions. This is crucial for trust and accountability.

Explainable AI (XAI): Developing AI systems that can explain their decision-making processes in a way that is understandable to humans. XAI is particularly important in sectors where AI decisions have significant impacts, such as healthcare, finance, and criminal justice.

Documentation and Reporting: Maintaining comprehensive documentation of AI systems, including their development process, data sources, and decision-making criteria, can enhance transparency.

Ethical AI Frameworks and Standards

The development and implementation of ethical frameworks and standards are essential for guiding AI development.

Adherence to Ethical Guidelines: Implementing existing ethical guidelines, such as the OECD Principles on AI or the EU Ethics Guidelines for Trustworthy AI (both shown overleaf), can help organisations develop and deploy AI responsibly.

Development of Industry-Specific Standards: Developing and adhering to industry-specific standards and practices can address sector-specific ethical concerns and challenges in AI deployment.

Stakeholder Engagement and Public Dialogue

Engaging with stakeholders and fostering public dialogue about AI is key to addressing ethical concerns.

Stakeholder Consultation: Regularly consulting with stakeholders, including users, consumers, ethicists, and regulators, can provide insights into the ethical implications of AI systems and how they might be addressed.

Public Education and Dialogue: Educating the public about AI and encouraging dialogue around its ethical use can help demystify AI and involve society in shaping its development.

Ensuring fairness and transparency in AI systems is not just a technical challenge but a societal imperative. By adopting these strategies, AI developers and users can contribute to the creation of AI systems that are not only effective but also equitable and trustworthy.

OECD Principles on AI

The OECD Principles on AI are a set of guidelines developed by the Organisation for Economic Co-operation and Development (OECD) to promote the responsible and trustworthy development and use of Artificial Intelligence (AI).

https://oecd.ai/en/ai-principles

Adopted in May 2019, these principles have been influential in shaping AI policies and practices globally. The principles are as follows:

1. **Inclusive Growth, Sustainable Development and Well-being:** AI should benefit people and the planet by driving inclusive growth, sustainable development, and well-being.

2. **Human-Centred Values and Fairness:** AI systems should respect human rights, democratic values, and diversity, and they should include appropriate safeguards – for example, enabling human intervention where necessary – to ensure a fair and just society.
3. **Transparency and Explainability:** There should be transparency and responsible disclosure around AI systems to ensure that people understand AI-based outcomes and can challenge them. This includes the need for AI systems to be explainable. Explainability is the capacity to express why an AI system reached a particular decision, recommendation, or prediction.
4. **Robustness, Security and Safety:** AI systems must function in a robust, secure, and safe way throughout their lifetimes, and potential risks should be continually assessed and managed.
5. **Accountability:** Organisations and individuals developing, deploying, or operating AI systems should be held accountable for their proper functioning in line with the above principles.

These principles are non-binding but are intended to provide a framework for governments and other stakeholders worldwide to responsibly steward AI technologies. They emphasise the importance of AI benefiting society at large, respecting human rights, and being developed and used in a transparent and accountable manner. Since their introduction, many countries and organisations have endorsed the

OECD AI Principles, reflecting a growing global consensus on the need for ethical guidelines in AI development and use.

EU Ethics Guidelines for Trustworthy AI

The EU Ethics Guidelines for Trustworthy AI were developed by the European Commission's High-Level Expert Group on Artificial Intelligence (AI HLEG). Released in April 2019, these guidelines provide a framework to ensure that AI systems are developed and used in a manner that is ethical and respects human rights and values. The guidelines define Trustworthy AI based on three components:

Lawful: AI should comply with all applicable laws and regulations.

Ethical: AI should adhere to ethical principles and values.

Robust: AI should be secure and reliable, both from a technical and social perspective.

The guidelines outline seven key requirements that AI systems should meet to be considered trustworthy:

1. **Human Agency and Oversight:** AI systems should support human autonomy and decision-making, as appropriate, and humans should be able to intervene in the operation of AI systems.

2. **Technical Robustness and Safety:** AI systems need to be resilient and secure. They should be safe and function correctly, with a minimal risk of unintended consequences.

3. **Privacy and Data Governance:** Individuals' privacy should be protected, and data collected by AI systems should be securely managed and processed.

4. **Transparency:** The capabilities and limitations of AI should be transparent and communicated clearly to users. The decision-making processes of AI systems should be understandable and traceable.

5. **Diversity, Non-discrimination, and Fairness:** AI systems should consider the full range of human abilities, skills, and requirements, and they should not discriminate against any individual or group.

6. **Societal and Environmental Well-being:** AI systems should benefit all human beings, including future generations, and should be environmentally sustainable.

7. **Accountability:** Mechanisms should be put in place to ensure responsibility and accountability for AI systems and their outcomes.

These guidelines aim to promote AI that is ethically sound, socially beneficial, and respects human rights. They are part of a broader effort by the European Union to establish a comprehensive AI strategy that balances innovation with ethical considerations and societal needs. The guidelines are intended to be a living document, evolving in response to new challenges and insights.

The Global AI Regulatory Landscape

As Artificial Intelligence (AI) continues to evolve and influence various sectors globally, understanding the diverse regulatory landscape becomes essential. This overview shows how different regions and countries approach AI governance, highlighting the varied perspectives and regulatory frameworks.

Diverse Approaches to AI Regulation

The approach to AI regulation varies significantly across the globe, reflecting diverse cultural, political, and economic contexts:

European Union (EU): The EU often leads in regulatory frameworks, focusing on privacy, data protection, and ethical standards. The GDPR and the proposed AI Act are key examples, emphasising human rights, transparency, and accountability.

United States (America): The U.S. approach is generally more market-driven, with less emphasis on regulation at the federal level and a stronger focus on technological innovation and competition. However, some states like California have introduced their own AI-related regulations.

China: China's approach is characterised by strong government support for AI development, aiming for global leadership in AI technology. Regulations focus on promoting AI growth while ensuring social stability and state security.

Other Regions: Countries like Japan, South Korea, Canada, and Australia have their own unique approaches, often balancing innovation with social and ethical considerations. These countries are also actively involved in international discussions on AI governance.

International Cooperation and Standards

Global Standards and Guidelines: There is a growing recognition of the need for international standards and cooperation in AI regulation. Organisations like the OECD, UNESCO, and the IEEE are actively working on global guidelines and standards for ethical AI.

Challenges in International Cooperation: Despite the need for global standards, achieving international consensus is challenging due to differing priorities, values, and political systems. Nevertheless, forums like the G7 and G20 are increasingly addressing AI governance.

Emerging Trends in Global AI Regulation

Focus on Ethical AI: Many countries are incorporating ethical considerations into their AI policies, emphasising principles like fairness, transparency, and accountability.

Sector-Specific Regulations: There is a trend towards developing sector-specific AI regulations, particularly in areas like healthcare, finance, and autonomous vehicles, where AI poses specific risks and opportunities.

Data Governance: With AI's reliance on data, many countries are focusing on data governance frameworks that balance innovation with privacy and security concerns.

The Role of National Strategies

National AI Strategies: Many countries have developed national AI strategies that outline their vision, goals, and action plans for AI. These strategies often include aspects of regulation, research and development, talent cultivation, and ethical considerations.

This highlights the varied and evolving regulatory landscape of AI across the globe. Understanding these differences is crucial for international AI development and collaboration. Each region's approach reflects its unique context and priorities, contributing to a diverse global perspective on AI governance.

Chapter 4:

Building an AI Strategy for Your Organisation

Assessing Organisational Readiness for AI

Before embarking on the journey of integrating Artificial Intelligence (AI) into business processes, an organisation must assess its readiness. These are key considerations and steps in evaluating an organisation's preparedness for adopting AI.

Understanding Current Capabilities

Technological Infrastructure: Evaluate the existing technological infrastructure to determine if it can support AI technologies. This includes hardware, software, and network capabilities.

Data Readiness: Assess the availability, quality, and structure of data since AI systems heavily rely on data for training and insights. Identify any gaps in data collection and management practices.

Evaluating Workforce Skills

AI Skills and Knowledge: Assess the level of AI expertise and knowledge within the organisation. Identify skill gaps and consider whether to develop these skills internally or seek external expertise.

Training and Development Needs: Plan for training programs to upskill existing staff, ensuring they can work effectively with AI technologies and understand their implications.

Organisational Culture and AI Adoption

Culture of Innovation: Evaluate the organisation's culture, especially its openness to innovation and change. A culture that encourages experimentation and adaptation is more conducive to successful AI integration.

Change Management: Consider the organisation's capacity for change management, as the adoption of AI may require significant shifts in workflows and processes.

Strategic Alignment

Alignment with Business Objectives: Ensure that the adoption of AI aligns with the overall business strategy and objectives. AI initiatives should support and enhance the organisation's strategic goals.

Identifying Use Cases: Identify potential AI use cases that can provide significant value to the organisation. Prioritise use cases based on their strategic alignment, feasibility, and potential impact.

Risk Assessment and Compliance

Legal and Ethical Considerations: Assess the legal and ethical implications of deploying AI, including data privacy, security, and compliance with relevant regulations.

Risk Management: Evaluate potential risks associated with AI adoption, including technological risks, operational disruptions, and reputational risks.

Financial and Resource Planning

Investment Requirements: Estimate the financial investment required for AI projects, including technology acquisition, talent development, and infrastructure upgrades.

Return on Investment (ROI) and other Performance Metrics: Define key performance indicators (KPIs) and expected return on investment (ROI) to measure the success of AI initiatives.

Assessing organisational readiness is a crucial first step in the AI adoption journey. It involves a comprehensive evaluation of technological capabilities, workforce skills, organisational culture, strategic alignment, risk management, and financial planning. By thoroughly assessing readiness, organisations can approach AI adoption with a clear understanding of their strengths, limitations, and areas needing improvement.

Defining Goals and Objectives

For any organisation looking to embrace Artificial Intelligence (AI), defining clear and strategic goals and objectives is essential as is understanding the process of setting focused, achievable aims for AI initiatives, ensuring alignment with the broader organisational strategy.

Understanding Organisational Needs and Opportunities

Needs Assessment: Begin by conducting a thorough assessment of the organisation's needs where AI could provide solutions. This involves identifying pain points, inefficiencies, or areas for improvement in current processes.

Opportunity Scoping: Look for opportunities where AI can add value, such as enhancing customer experience, improving operational efficiency, or creating new business models.

Aligning AI Goals with Business Strategy

Strategic Alignment: Ensure that the goals for AI are aligned with the overall business strategy and objectives. AI initiatives should support and contribute to the organisation's strategic vision and long-term plans.

Stakeholder Engagement: Involve key stakeholders from various departments in defining AI goals. This inclusive approach ensures that the AI strategy addresses a wide range of organisational needs and gains broad support.

Setting Specific and Measurable Objectives

SMART Objectives: Set Specific, Measurable, Achievable, Relevant, and Time-bound (SMART) objectives for AI projects. This approach helps in creating clear and actionable goals, facilitating better planning and evaluation.

Prioritisation of Objectives: Given the resources and time required for AI projects, prioritise objectives based on potential impact, feasibility, and alignment with strategic goals.

Establishing Key Performance Indicators (KPIs)

Defining KPIs: Establish KPIs to measure the success and impact of AI initiatives. These should be linked to the defined objectives and capable of providing insights into the performance of AI solutions.

Continuous Monitoring and Adjustment: Plan for regular monitoring of these KPIs and be prepared to adjust objectives and strategies based on performance and evolving organisational needs.

Risk Assessment and Mitigation

Identifying Risks: As part of goal setting, identify potential risks associated with AI initiatives, including technical, operational, ethical, and reputational risks.

Mitigation Strategies: Develop strategies to mitigate these risks, ensuring that objectives are achievable and sustainable.

Developing a Roadmap for Implementation

Phased Approach: Develop a phased roadmap for AI implementation, outlining the progression from initial pilot projects to broader deployment. This allows for learning and adjustments along the way.

Resource Allocation: Ensure that necessary resources, including budget, personnel, and technology, are allocated in line with the defined objectives and roadmap.

Defining clear goals and objectives is crucial for the successful integration of AI into organisational processes. It ensures that AI initiatives are focused, strategically aligned, and capable of delivering measurable benefits. Proper goal setting also facilitates effective planning, resource allocation, and risk management in AI projects.

Aligning AI with Business Strategy

Integrating Artificial Intelligence (AI) into an organisation's business strategy is key to leveraging its full potential. It is important to align AI initiatives with overall business goals and strategies, ensuring that AI contributes meaningfully to the organisation's success.

Understanding Business Goals and Challenges

Assessing Business Objectives: Begin by thoroughly understanding the organisation's long-term goals and current challenges. This understanding will guide where and how AI can be most effectively implemented.

Identifying AI Opportunities: Identify areas within the business strategy where AI can play a transformative role. This could include improving customer experiences, optimising operations, or driving innovation.

Strategic Integration of AI

Seamless Integration: AI should not be viewed as a standalone tool but as an integral part of the strategic planning process. Ensure that AI initiatives are embedded within the business strategy, complementing, and enhancing existing efforts.

Cross-Functional Collaboration: Foster collaboration across different departments to ensure AI initiatives are well-integrated with various aspects of the business. This helps in creating a unified approach where AI supports diverse business functions.

Customising AI to Business Needs

Tailored AI Solutions: Avoid one-size-fits-all AI solutions. Customise AI applications to address specific business needs and challenges, ensuring they are relevant and add value to existing processes.

Scalability and Flexibility: Plan for AI solutions that are scalable and flexible, allowing them to evolve with the changing needs of the business and advancements in AI technology.

Aligning AI with Business Culture

Cultural Alignment: Ensure that the AI strategy is in harmony with the organisation's culture. AI initiatives should support and be supported by the organisational values, practices, and people.

Change Management: Incorporate effective change management strategies to help employees adapt to AI-enhanced processes and understand the benefits of AI in their work.

Measuring and Evaluating AI Impact

Setting Metrics for Success: Define clear metrics to measure the impact of AI on business outcomes. These should be aligned with the broader business objectives.

Continuous Evaluation: Regularly evaluate the performance of AI initiatives against these metrics and adjust strategies as needed for continuous improvement.

Staying Agile and Future-Focused

Agility in Strategy: Maintain agility in AI strategy to adapt to new opportunities and changes in the business environment.

Futureproofing: Keep an eye on emerging AI trends and technologies to ensure the business stays ahead of the curve and ready to adapt to future developments in AI.

Aligning AI with business strategy is crucial for maximising the benefits of AI technologies. It involves a holistic approach where AI initiatives are seamlessly integrated with the business goals, culture, and operations. This alignment ensures that AI not only supports but also enhances the strategic objectives of the organisation.

Developing a Roadmap for AI Implementation

Creating a structured and strategic roadmap is essential for the successful implementation of Artificial Intelligence (AI) in an organisation. It is vital to develop a comprehensive plan that guides the AI adoption process, from initial conception to full-scale deployment.

Initial Assessment and Planning

Understanding the AI Landscape: Begin with a thorough assessment of the AI technologies relevant to your business needs and goals. This includes understanding the capabilities and limitations of different AI solutions.

Identifying Pilot Projects: Select pilot projects that are manageable in scope and have the potential to provide quick wins or valuable insights. Pilots serve as a testbed for larger-scale implementations.

Setting Clear Milestones and Timelines

Phased Approach: Develop a phased approach for AI implementation. Outline clear milestones and timelines for each phase, from pilot testing and evaluation to broader rollouts.

Flexibility in Planning: While having a structured plan is important, maintaining flexibility to adapt to unforeseen challenges or shifts in technology and business priorities is equally crucial.

Resource Allocation and Management

Budgeting for AI Projects: Allocate a budget for each phase of the AI implementation. Consider not only the direct costs of technology and tools but also the indirect costs such as training, change management, and potential disruptions.

Team and Resource Planning: Identify the team members and resources required for each phase. This might include AI specialists, data scientists, project managers, and cross-functional team members.

Planning How to Use AI in Your Organisation

Many people buy this book because of seeing one of my Harnessing AI talks or participating in one of my Leadership Team masterclasses, in those I often refer to the nine planning steps.

This is a robust and comprehensive approach to integrating Artificial Intelligence (AI) into a business environment. It encompasses critical steps that ensure a thoughtful and effective adoption of AI technology. The nine steps are as follows:

1. **Identify Business Goals and Needs Assessment:** Begin by clearly defining your business goals and conducting a thorough needs assessment to understand how AI can address specific challenges or opportunities within your organisation. This ensures that the AI

solution aligns with specific business objectives, making the investment more targeted and effective.

2. **Research AI Types for Specific Needs:** Investigate various types of AI technologies to determine which aligns best with your business needs, focusing on their capabilities and potential applications. This step is crucial for understanding the landscape of AI technologies and selecting the right tool for your specific business needs, avoiding costly mismatches.

3. **Benchmarking with Industry Peers:** Investigate how other organisations in your sector are leveraging AI. This can provide insights into successful strategies and common pitfalls to avoid. Learning from the experiences of others in your sector can provide valuable insights into best practices and help you anticipate potential challenges.

4. **Feasibility Study:** Assess the feasibility of implementing AI in your business by evaluating the data you have available, the costs involved, and the technical

infrastructure required. This step assesses the practicality of implementing AI in your organisation, considering your current data infrastructure and budget constraints, which is essential for a successful deployment.

5. **Strategic Partner Selection:** Identify and choose strategic partners or vendors who have the expertise and experience to help you implement AI solutions effectively. Choosing the right partners or vendors can significantly influence the success of your AI projects, given the complexity and specialised nature of AI technologies.

6. **Pilot Test and ROI Analysis:** Conduct a pilot test of the chosen AI solution to evaluate its impact and understand the return on investment (ROI) it offers, ensuring it aligns with your business objectives. Testing the AI solution on a smaller scale initially helps identify any issues before a full rollout and provides a clearer picture of the potential return on investment.

7. **Implementation, Monitoring, and Tweaking:** After the pilot, move forward

with full implementation. Continuously monitor the AI system's performance and make necessary adjustments to optimise its effectiveness. Continuous monitoring and the ability to make adjustments post-implementation are key to ensuring that the AI system evolves and remains aligned with business goals.

8. **Training and Stakeholder Consideration:** Ensure that employees at all levels are properly trained to work with the new AI system. Also, consider the impact of AI implementation on all stakeholders, including customers and employees. Proper training is essential for user adoption and effective use of AI technology. Considering the impact on all stakeholders ensures a smooth transition and broad support.

9. **Continuous Improvement and Retraining:** AI systems require ongoing maintenance and updates to stay effective. Continually improve and update the AI application as needed and retrain the system with new data to maintain its relevance and accuracy. AI is not a 'set and forget' solution. It requires ongoing attention and updates to stay

effective, especially as business needs and the external environment change.

Risk Management and Contingency Planning

Identifying Risks: Assess potential risks at each stage of the AI implementation process. Risks could include technical challenges, data privacy concerns, and user resistance.

Developing Contingency Plans: Create contingency plans for identified risks. Ensure there are strategies in place to mitigate potential setbacks.

Integration with Business Processes

Seamless Integration: Plan for the seamless integration of AI into existing business processes. This includes ensuring compatibility with existing systems and workflows.

Change Management: Incorporate change management strategies to facilitate the adoption of

AI within the organisation. Prepare for organisational changes that AI implementation might necessitate.

Continuous Monitoring and Evaluation

Performance Monitoring: Establish mechanisms for continuous monitoring of AI systems. Regularly evaluate AI performance against set objectives and KPIs.

Iterative Improvement: Use insights gained from performance monitoring for iterative improvements. Be prepared to refine and adjust the AI strategy based on feedback and results.

Scalability and Future Expansion

Planning for Scale: Design the AI implementation roadmap with scalability in mind. Consider how AI solutions can be expanded or adapted as the organisation grows and evolves.

Staying Informed on AI Advancements: Keep abreast of ongoing advancements in AI to identify opportunities for further implementation or improvement.

A well-crafted AI implementation roadmap is a critical tool for guiding organisations through the complexities of AI adoption. It offers a clear, step-by-step guide to navigating the AI journey, ensuring that each phase is thoughtfully planned and executed.

Risk Management and Mitigation in AI Projects

Effective risk management is crucial for the successful implementation of Artificial Intelligence (AI) in any organisation. The identification and mitigation of the various risks associated with AI projects is imperative.

Identifying Potential Risks

Technical Risks: These include challenges related to data quality, algorithm performance, integration with existing systems, and scalability of AI solutions.

Operational Risks: Operational risks may arise from disruptions to business processes during AI implementation, potential downtime, or inefficiencies during the transition phase.

Ethical and Legal Risks: Ethical risks involve issues related to bias, transparency, and decision-making processes in AI systems. Legal risks encompass compliance with data protection and privacy laws, intellectual property rights, and other relevant regulations.

Reputational Risks: The use of AI can impact an organisation's reputation, especially if AI-driven decisions lead to public controversies or if there are perceived issues of fairness or privacy infringement.

Developing a Risk Mitigation Strategy

Comprehensive Risk Assessment: Conduct a thorough risk assessment at the outset of any AI project. Understand the potential impact of each risk on the project and the organisation.

Mitigation Plans: Develop specific mitigation strategies for each identified risk. This could include technical solutions, operational adjustments, legal compliance checks, and ethical reviews.

Involving Cross-Functional Teams: Engage cross-functional teams in risk assessment and mitigation planning, ensuring a holistic approach that encompasses various aspects of the organisation.

Ensuring Data Privacy and Security

Robust Data Governance: Implement robust data governance practices to manage the risks associated with data privacy and security. This includes adherence to data protection regulations, data anonymisation techniques, and secure data storage and transmission.

Regular Security Audits: Conduct regular security audits of AI systems to identify and address potential vulnerabilities.

Continuous Monitoring and Evaluation

Real-Time Monitoring: Establish real-time monitoring mechanisms to detect and address risks promptly as they arise during the AI project lifecycle.

Feedback Loops: Create feedback loops that allow for continuous learning and improvement in risk management strategies based on actual project experiences and outcomes.

Training and Awareness

Staff Training: Train staff on the potential risks associated with AI projects and the importance of adherence to risk mitigation strategies.

Stakeholder Awareness: Ensure that all stakeholders, including leadership, project teams, and end-users, are aware of the potential risks and their roles in mitigating them.

Preparing for Ethical Considerations

Ethical AI Framework: Develop and adhere to an ethical AI framework that guides decision-making processes in AI development and use.

Regular Ethical Reviews: Conduct regular ethical reviews of AI projects to ensure they align with organisational values and societal norms.

Risk management in AI projects is a multi-faceted process that requires careful planning, continuous monitoring, and proactive mitigation strategies. By effectively managing risks, organisations can ensure the smooth implementation and operation of AI systems, maintaining trust and integrity throughout the process.

Chapter 5:
Developing AI Capabilities

Building or Acquiring AI Talent

As organisations embrace Artificial Intelligence (AI), one of the key challenges they face is building or acquiring the necessary talent to drive their AI initiatives. There are several strategies to consider for developing AI capabilities within the workforce and several options for acquiring external AI expertise.

Assessing Talent Needs

Skills Gap Analysis: Analyse the workforce to identify the specific AI skills and expertise needed in the organisation. This includes technical skills like data science and machine learning, as well as domain-specific knowledge.

Future Talent Planning: Forecast future talent needs based on the organisation's long-term AI strategy. Consider how evolving AI technologies might shape these requirements.

Building AI Talent Internally

Training and Upskilling Programs: Invest in training and upskilling current employees. This can include workshops, courses, and certifications in AI-related fields. There are various suggested sources in the appendices of this book.

Mentorship and Collaboration: Foster a culture of learning by setting up mentorship programs and encouraging collaboration between AI experts and other employees.

Career Development Paths: Create clear career paths for AI roles, providing employees with opportunities for growth and advancement in this area.

Acquiring AI Talent Externally

Hiring Specialists: When specific expertise is not available internally, look to hire AI specialists. This includes data scientists, AI engineers, and domain experts with AI experience.

Partnering with Academia and Research Institutions: Establish partnerships with universities, colleges and research institutions. This can provide access to innovative AI research and a pool of talent.

Utilising Freelancers and Consultants: For short-term needs or specific projects, consider hiring freelancers or consultants who can bring in specialised AI expertise.

Cultivating an AI-Ready Culture

Promoting AI Literacy: Ensure that all employees, not just technical staff, have a basic understanding of AI and its implications for the business. Organise workshops or staff briefings from industry professionals but do ensure that they position the subject appropriately for the audience.

Encouraging Innovation and Experimentation: Foster a workplace culture that encourages innovation and experimentation with AI technologies.

Diversity and Inclusion in AI Talent

Diverse Talent Acquisition: Actively seek diverse talent in AI recruitment to bring varied perspectives and reduce biases in AI systems.

Inclusive AI Teams: Create inclusive environments where people from different backgrounds can contribute effectively to AI projects.

Balancing Internal and External Talent Strategies

Strategic Balance: Find the right balance between building internal capabilities and leveraging external expertise. This balance will depend on factors like the scale of AI projects, budget constraints, and long-term strategic goals.

Building or acquiring AI talent is a critical step in an organisation's journey towards AI maturity. It requires a strategic approach to identify skill gaps, invest in training and development, and attract the right talent, all while fostering a culture conducive to AI innovation.

Choosing the Right AI Technologies and Tools

For organisations venturing into Artificial Intelligence (AI), selecting the appropriate technologies and tools is a pivotal decision. Here we discuss the factors to consider and the process for choosing AI technologies that align with organisational needs and goals.

Understanding Business Requirements

Assessment of Needs: Start by assessing the specific needs of your organisation. Understand the problems or challenges that AI is expected to address. Understand what you are aiming to achieve. Are you looking to improve customer service, automate repetitive tasks, or glean insights from data?

Alignment with Business Goals: Ensure that the chosen AI technologies are in line with the business's strategic objectives. AI should be a means to enhance business outcomes, and not an end in itself.

Evaluating AI Technologies

Technical Suitability: Evaluate AI technologies for their technical suitability to your business requirements. This includes considering the type of AI (e.g., machine learning, natural language processing, computer vision) and its applicability to your use cases.

Scalability and Integration: Assess the scalability of the AI solutions and their compatibility with existing systems and infrastructure. The chosen technology should integrate smoothly with current business processes and systems.

Vendor Assessment and Selection

Reputation and Reliability: Research vendors' reputations and track records. Look for case studies or references from other clients, especially those in similar industries.

Support and Services: Consider the level of support and services offered by the vendor, including training, maintenance, and customer service.

Cost Considerations: Analyse the cost implications of different AI technologies and tools. This includes not only the initial investment but also long-term costs such as licenses, updates, and support.

Trial and Evaluation

Proof of Concept: Before full-scale implementation, conduct a proof of concept or pilot project. This allows you to evaluate the technology's effectiveness and suitability for your specific needs.

Feedback and Iteration: Gather feedback from users and stakeholders during the trial phase. Use this feedback to make iterative improvements or changes to your AI technology choice.

Staying Informed on AI Advancements

Continuous Learning: The field of AI is rapidly evolving. Stay informed about the latest advancements and emerging technologies that could benefit your business.

Networking and Industry Events: Participate in industry events, seminars, and online forums. Networking with peers can provide insights into effective AI solutions and trends.

Considering Ethical and Legal Implications

Ethical Considerations: Ensure that the AI technologies and tools align with ethical standards, particularly regarding data privacy, bias, and transparency.

Regulatory Compliance: Be aware of and comply with relevant regulations and laws that apply to the AI technologies you are considering.

Choosing the right AI technologies and tools is a critical step that requires careful consideration of business needs, technical capabilities, vendor selection, and ethical implications. A thoughtful and well-informed approach can significantly enhance the likelihood of successful AI implementation.

Creating a Culture of Innovation and AI Adoption

For Artificial Intelligence (AI) to be successfully integrated and utilised within an organisation, fostering a culture that embraces innovation and AI adoption is essential. Consider these strategies for cultivating an environment conducive to embracing AI technologies.

Promoting AI Literacy Across the Organisation

Educational Initiatives: Implement educational programs to enhance AI literacy across all levels of the organisation. This includes workshops, seminars, and training sessions that demystify AI and convey its potential benefits.

Accessible Learning Resources: Provide accessible resources, such as online courses and internal knowledge-sharing platforms, to encourage self-learning and exploration of AI.

Encouraging a Mindset of Innovation

Innovation as a Core Value: Embed innovation as a core value in the organisation's culture. Encourage employees to think creatively and be open to experimenting with new technologies.

Supporting Experimentation: Create a safe environment for experimentation where failures are viewed as learning opportunities. This approach fosters an innovative mindset and willingness to try new things.

Leadership and Management Support

Leadership Endorsement: Ensure strong endorsement and support for AI initiatives from top management. Leadership can set the tone for AI adoption by articulating its importance and aligning it with business goals.

Change Champions: Identify and empower 'change champions' within the organisation who can advocate for and guide AI initiatives. These individuals can be pivotal in driving enthusiasm and acceptance of AI.

Incentivising AI Adoption

Reward Systems: Implement reward systems that recognise and celebrate successes in AI projects and initiatives. Acknowledge both team and individual contributions to foster a sense of ownership and achievement.

Career Advancement Opportunities: Provide clear pathways for career advancement that are tied to AI skill development and implementation, incentivising employees to engage with AI technologies.

Fostering Collaboration and Cross-Functional Teams

Interdepartmental Collaboration: Encourage collaboration across different departments and teams in AI projects. This promotes a holistic approach to AI implementation, leveraging diverse perspectives and expertise.

Community Building: Build a community of AI enthusiasts within the organisation who can share ideas, experiences, and best practices. This can include regular meetups, internal conferences, or online forums.

Managing the Impact of AI on Workforce

Addressing Job Security Concerns: Transparently address any concerns about job displacement due to AI. Focus on the narrative of AI as a tool for augmentation rather than replacement.

Reskilling and Upskilling Initiatives: Invest in reskilling and upskilling programs to prepare the workforce for changes brought about by AI. Equip employees with skills to work alongside AI technologies effectively.

Creating a culture of innovation and AI adoption is key to realising the full potential of AI within an organisation. It involves educating the workforce, fostering a mindset open to innovation, providing strong leadership support, incentivising AI adoption, encouraging collaboration, and responsibly managing workforce transitions.

Integrating AI into Business Processes

Successfully integrating Artificial Intelligence (AI) into existing business processes is crucial for maximising its benefits and ensuring seamless operation. Adopting these strategies will help you embed AI effectively within an organisation's workflows and systems.

Assessment and Identification of Integration Points

Process Mapping: Begin with a detailed mapping of existing business processes to identify potential areas for AI integration. Focus on processes that can benefit most from automation, data analysis, and intelligent decision-making.

Feasibility Analysis: Conduct a feasibility analysis for integrating AI into these processes. Consider factors like the potential for improvement, data availability, and the technical complexity of integration.

Customising AI Solutions to Fit Business Needs

Tailored AI Implementation: Customise AI solutions to meet the specific needs and nuances of your business processes. Avoid a one-size-fits-all approach; instead, adapt AI technologies to complement and enhance existing workflows.

User-Centric Design: Design AI systems with the end-user in mind. Ensure that AI tools are user-friendly and intuitive and add value to the employees' daily tasks.

Ensuring Smooth Integration and Minimising Disruption

Gradual Implementation: Implement AI solutions gradually to minimise disruption. Start with smaller projects or pilot programs before scaling up to larger deployments.

Integration with Existing Systems: Ensure that AI solutions integrate smoothly with existing IT systems and infrastructure. Compatibility and interoperability are key to effective AI integration.

Employee Training and Support

Training Programs: Provide comprehensive training for employees who will be using or interacting with AI systems. This training should cover not only how to use the systems but also how to interpret and act on AI-generated insights.

Ongoing Support: Establish a support system to assist employees as they adapt to AI-integrated processes. This can include help desks, user guides, and regular check-ins.

Monitoring and Continuous Improvement

Performance Tracking: Monitor the performance of AI-integrated processes to assess their impact. Use metrics and KPIs to measure improvements in efficiency, accuracy, and other relevant factors.

Feedback Loops: Create feedback loops to gather insights from employees and users of AI systems. Use this feedback to make continuous improvements and adjustments.

Addressing Ethical and Compliance Considerations

Ethical Guidelines: Ensure that AI integration adheres to ethical guidelines, particularly in terms of transparency, fairness, and privacy.

Regulatory Compliance: Stay compliant with relevant industry regulations and standards when integrating AI into business processes.

Integrating AI into business processes requires careful planning, customisation to fit specific business needs, employee training and support, continuous monitoring, and a strong commitment to ethical and regulatory compliance. When done effectively, AI can significantly enhance business efficiency, decision-making, and overall performance.

Building Sustainable AI Systems

Developing sustainable AI systems is crucial for ensuring long-term viability and alignment with broader environmental, ethical, and business goals. Please consider these strategies for building AI systems that are sustainable in terms of technology, ethics, and business practices.

Ensuring Technological Sustainability

Scalability: Design AI systems that are scalable and can adapt to growing or changing business needs. This includes considering the future expansion of data sources, user base, and functionality.

Maintainability: Focus on the maintainability of AI systems, ensuring they are easy to update, modify, and manage over time. This involves using modular designs, clear documentation, and standard coding practices.

Environmental Considerations

Energy Efficiency: Optimise AI algorithms and infrastructure for energy efficiency, especially for large-scale AI models and data centres. Consider the environmental impact of your AI systems and strive for greener alternatives.

Resource Optimisation: Utilise AI itself to optimise resource use in operations, potentially reducing waste and improving overall environmental sustainability.

Ethical AI Development

Responsible Data Use: Implement responsible data practices, ensuring that AI systems use data ethically, respect user privacy, and comply with data protection regulations.

Bias Mitigation: Continuously work on identifying and mitigating biases in AI systems. This includes regularly auditing AI models and using diverse datasets for training.

Aligning with Business and Societal Goals

Alignment with Business Values: Ensure that AI systems align with the core values and objectives of the organisation. AI should support strategic business goals and enhance rather than detract from the organisation's mission.

Contribution to Society: Consider how your AI systems can contribute positively to society. This might involve addressing social challenges, improving accessibility, or enhancing public services.

Stakeholder Engagement and Transparency

Involving Stakeholders: Engage with various stakeholders, including customers, employees, and the wider community, in the development of AI systems. This ensures that the systems are well-rounded and consider diverse perspectives.

Transparent Operations: Maintain transparency about how AI systems operate, the data they use, and the decision-making processes involved. This builds trust and accountability.

Fostering a Culture of Continuous Learning

Adaptability to New Developments: Encourage a culture of continuous learning and adaptability within the organisation to keep up with the rapid developments in AI.

Feedback Mechanisms: Implement mechanisms for regular feedback and learning from AI deployments, using insights gained to improve and evolve the AI systems sustainably.

Building sustainable AI systems is about more than just technological development; it encompasses ethical considerations, environmental impact, and alignment with long-term business and societal goals. A sustainable approach ensures that AI systems remain effective, relevant, and responsible over time.

Chapter 6:
Implementing AI Projects

Project Management Techniques for AI Initiatives

Effective project management is crucial for the success of Artificial Intelligence (AI) initiatives. Here I offer outlines of key project management techniques tailored to the unique challenges and characteristics of AI projects.

Defining Scope and Objectives

Clear Project Scope: Clearly define the scope of the AI project, including its objectives, deliverables, and boundaries. This helps in setting realistic expectations and aligning the project with business goals.

Objectives Alignment: Ensure that the project objectives are aligned with the strategic goals of the organisation and have measurable outcomes.

Agile Methodology in AI Projects

Flexibility and Adaptability: Given the experimental and evolving nature of AI, adopting an agile methodology can be particularly effective. This approach allows for flexibility, quick iterations, and adaptability to change.

Incremental Development: Break down the project into smaller, manageable increments or sprints. This facilitates continuous evaluation and adjustment based on feedback and outcomes.

Stakeholder Engagement and Communication

Regular Stakeholder Updates: Keep all stakeholders informed about the project's progress, challenges, and changes. Transparent and regular communication is key to managing expectations and garnering support.

Cross-Functional Collaboration: Encourage collaboration between different teams, such as data scientists, IT professionals, and domain experts, to leverage diverse skills and perspectives.

Risk Management in AI Projects

Risk Identification and Assessment: Identify potential risks specific to AI projects, such as data quality issues, model inaccuracies, and ethical concerns. Assess the likelihood and impact of these risks.

Mitigation Strategies: Develop strategies to mitigate identified risks. This could include contingency plans, risk transfer methods, or risk acceptance where appropriate.

Resource Management

Effective Resource Allocation: Allocate resources efficiently, including budget, personnel, and technology. Consider the unique requirements of AI projects, such as high computational resources for model training.

Skillset Alignment: Ensure that the team has the right mix of skills. This might involve training existing staff, hiring new talent, or partnering with external experts.

Performance Monitoring and Evaluation

Tracking Progress: Implement tools and metrics to track the progress of the AI project against its objectives. This includes monitoring the development of AI models, data preparation, and integration with existing systems.

Iterative Improvement: Use performance data to make iterative improvements in the project. AI projects often require continuous refinement and tuning of models based on real-world feedback and results.

Effective project management for AI initiatives requires a blend of traditional techniques and approaches tailored to the unique aspects of AI. Emphasising agility, stakeholder engagement, risk management, and continuous improvement is key to navigating the complexities and uncertainties of AI projects.

Overcoming Common Challenges in AI Implementation

Implementing Artificial Intelligence (AI) in an organisation often comes with a unique set of challenges. These are common obstacles often encountered with AI projects, but these strategies will help to overcome them.

Data-Related Challenges

Data Quality and Quantity: Ensure access to high-quality and relevant data in sufficient quantities. Overcome this by improving data collection processes, augmenting datasets, or using data augmentation techniques.

Data Privacy and Security: Address privacy and security concerns by implementing robust data governance policies and complying with data protection regulations.

Integration with Existing Systems

Technical Compatibility: Overcome integration challenges by ensuring AI solutions are compatible with existing systems. This may involve using APIs, custom integration solutions, or upgrading legacy systems.

Minimising Disruption: Plan the integration process to minimise disruption to existing workflows. This could include phased rollouts and providing adequate support during the transition period.

Managing Expectations

Setting Realistic Expectations: Manage expectations by communicating the capabilities and limitations of AI clearly to stakeholders. Avoid overselling AI capabilities and set realistic timelines.

Demonstrating Value Early: Implement pilot projects or proof-of-concept initiatives to demonstrate early wins and the potential value of AI.

Talent and Expertise Gaps

Building Internal Expertise: Address talent gaps by investing in training and upskilling existing employees, or by hiring AI specialists.

External Partnerships: Consider partnering with external AI vendors, consultants, or academic institutions to access specialised AI expertise.

Ethical and Legal Considerations

Addressing Ethical Concerns: Implement ethical AI practices, including transparency, fairness, and accountability in AI systems. Regularly conduct ethical audits of AI systems.

Legal Compliance: Stay informed about and comply with relevant legal and regulatory requirements related to AI.

Change Management

Fostering Organisational Buy-In: Secure buy-in from leadership and key stakeholders. Highlight the strategic importance of AI and its alignment with organisational goals.

Preparing the Workforce: Prepare the workforce for AI integration through training and awareness programs. Address concerns about job displacement by focusing on AI as a tool for augmentation.

Continuous Monitoring and Iteration

Feedback Loops: Establish feedback mechanisms to continuously gather insights from AI system users and stakeholders.

Iterative Development: Adopt an iterative approach to AI implementation, allowing for adjustments and improvements based on feedback and performance metrics.

Overcoming the challenges in AI implementation requires a strategic approach, focusing on data management, system integration, managing expectations, addressing talent gaps, and ensuring ethical and legal compliance. Effective change management and continuous iteration are also vital for successful AI adoption.

Case Studies of Successful AI Projects

Analysing real-world examples of successful AI implementations can provide valuable insights and lessons for organisations looking to embark on their AI journey. Below are a series of case studies highlighting the successful application of AI across various industries.

Case Study 1: Retail Industry - Personalised Customer Experiences

Overview: A leading retail company implemented an AI-powered recommendation system to personalise shopping experiences for its customers.

Implementation: The system used customer data and machine learning algorithms to predict preferences and suggest products.

Outcome: The result was a significant increase in customer engagement and sales, demonstrating the power of AI in enhancing customer experience.

Case Study 2: Healthcare - Predictive Analytics for Patient Care

Overview: A healthcare provider used AI to predict patient risks and improve care management.
Implementation: The AI system analysed patient records and real-time health data to identify patients at risk of chronic diseases.
Outcome: Early intervention strategies were developed, improving patient outcomes, and reducing hospital readmission rates.

Case Study 3: Financial Services - Fraud Detection

Overview: A financial institution integrated AI into its fraud detection system to identify and prevent fraudulent transactions.
Implementation: The system employed deep learning techniques to analyse transaction patterns and detect anomalies.
Outcome: The AI-enhanced system reduced false positives and identified fraudulent activities more accurately, saving the company millions in potential losses.

Case Study 4: Manufacturing - Predictive Maintenance

Overview: A manufacturing company implemented AI for predictive maintenance of its equipment.
Implementation: Using sensors and AI algorithms, the system predicted equipment failures before they occurred.
Outcome: This proactive approach reduced downtime, extended equipment life, and optimised maintenance schedules.

Case Study 5: Agriculture - AI in Crop Management

Overview: An agricultural firm used AI to optimise crop yields and reduce resource usage.
Implementation: AI algorithms analysed weather data, soil conditions, and crop growth patterns to provide actionable insights.
Outcome: The AI-driven approach led to more efficient use of water and fertilisers, higher crop yields, and reduced environmental impact.

Lessons Learned

Each of these case studies demonstrates how AI can be effectively applied to solve real-world problems and deliver tangible benefits. Key lessons include the importance of:

Clear Objective Setting: Defining clear goals and objectives for AI projects.

Data Quality and Management: Ensuring access to high-quality data and robust data management practices.

Stakeholder Engagement: Involving key stakeholders throughout the AI project lifecycle.

Ethical and Responsible AI Use: Considering the ethical implications of AI solutions and ensuring responsible use.

These case studies provide insights into the practical application of AI across different sectors, showcasing the diverse ways AI can drive innovation, efficiency, and value creation.

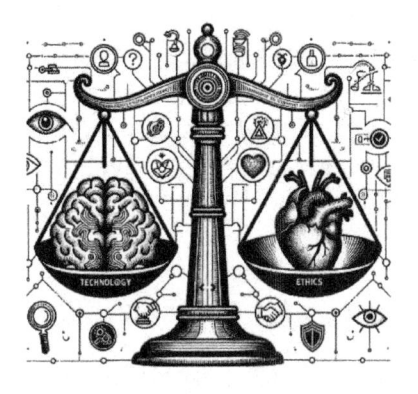

Ensuring Ethical and Responsible AI Implementation

As Artificial Intelligence (AI) becomes more integrated into various aspects of business and society, ensuring its ethical and responsible implementation is paramount. These are the key considerations and practices necessary to uphold ethical standards in AI initiatives.

Developing Ethical AI Guidelines

Framework for Ethical AI: Establish a comprehensive set of guidelines or a framework to ensure AI is developed and used ethically. This should include principles such as fairness, accountability, transparency, and respect for user privacy.

Incorporating Stakeholder Input: Involve a diverse range of stakeholders in developing these guidelines, including ethicists, legal experts, AI technologists, and representatives from affected communities.

Transparency and Explainability

Understanding AI Decisions: Strive for transparency in AI decision-making processes. This involves making AI systems as explainable as possible, particularly in sectors where decisions have significant impacts, such as healthcare and finance.

Communicating AI Processes: Communicate how AI systems work, the data they use, and their decision-making processes to all stakeholders, including end-users and employees.

Bias Detection and Mitigation

Proactive Identification of Biases: Regularly audit and test AI systems for biases. This includes examining training data, algorithms, and output decisions for any form of bias or discrimination.

Continuous Improvement: Implement processes for continuous monitoring and improvement of AI systems to mitigate biases and ensure they function as intended.

Data Privacy and Security

Robust Data Practices: Adhere to strict data privacy and security practices. Ensure compliance with data protection laws like GDPR, employing practices like data anonymisation and secure data storage.

Consent and User Rights: Respect user rights by obtaining explicit consent for data collection and use, and providing users with control over their data.

Accountability and Governance

Clear Accountability Structures: Establish clear accountability structures for AI decision-making. This includes defining who is responsible for the outcomes of AI systems and setting up governance mechanisms to oversee AI implementations.

Ethical AI Audits: Conduct regular ethical audits of AI projects to ensure ongoing compliance with ethical guidelines and legal standards.

Risk Assessment and Management

Comprehensive Risk Analysis: Perform comprehensive risk analyses to identify potential ethical and societal risks associated with AI implementations.

Mitigation Strategies: Develop and implement strategies to mitigate identified risks, including contingency plans for scenarios where AI systems may not perform as expected.

Stakeholder Education and Engagement

Educational Programs: Develop educational programs to raise awareness about the ethical aspects of AI among employees and stakeholders.

Public Engagement: Engage with the public and industry peers to promote discussions around ethical AI, sharing best practices and learning from others.

Ensuring ethical and responsible AI implementation is a multifaceted effort that requires careful planning, continuous monitoring, and a commitment to upholding high ethical standards. It involves not only technical considerations but also a broader understanding of AI's societal impacts.

Post-Implementation: Monitoring and Maintenance of AI Systems

After the implementation of Artificial Intelligence (AI) systems, ongoing monitoring and maintenance are crucial to ensure their continued effectiveness and alignment with business objectives. Post-implementation, these are the key practices for managing AI systems.

Continuous Monitoring for Performance and Accuracy

Performance Tracking: Regularly monitor the performance of AI systems against predefined metrics and objectives. This includes tracking accuracy, efficiency, and any other relevant performance indicators.

Real-Time Monitoring Systems: Implement real-time monitoring tools to promptly detect and address performance issues or deviations from expected outcomes.

Regular Updates and Model Retraining

Updating AI Models: AI models can become outdated as data patterns and external conditions change. Plan for regular updates and retraining of models with new data to maintain their accuracy and relevance.

Adapting to Changes: Be prepared to adapt AI systems to changes in the business environment, regulatory landscape, or technological advancements.

Maintenance and Technical Support

Routine Maintenance: Establish routine maintenance schedules for AI systems, including software updates, security patches, and checks for data integrity.

Technical Support Team: Maintain a dedicated technical support team to address issues, provide user support, and manage maintenance tasks.

User Feedback and Iterative Improvement

Gathering User Feedback: Actively gather and analyse feedback from users of the AI systems. User insights can be invaluable in identifying areas for improvement.

Iterative Development: Use feedback and performance data to make iterative improvements to AI systems, enhancing their functionality and user experience.

Ethical and Compliance Audits

Regular Ethical Reviews: Conduct regular audits to ensure that AI systems continue to adhere to ethical standards and guidelines. This includes monitoring for biases, privacy concerns, and transparency.

Compliance Checks: Regularly review AI systems for compliance with relevant laws, regulations, and industry standards. This is particularly important for sectors with stringent regulatory requirements.

Documentation and Knowledge Management

Up-to-Date Documentation: Keep comprehensive documentation for AI systems, including technical specifications, user guides, and maintenance logs.

Knowledge Sharing: Foster knowledge sharing practices within the organisation to ensure a broad understanding of AI systems and their operations.

Managing Scalability and Future Integration

Scalability Planning: Plan for the scalability of AI systems to accommodate business growth or increased data volumes.

Future Integration Prospects: Stay open to integrating AI systems with new technologies or business systems that may emerge in the future.

Post-implementation management of AI systems is a critical phase where the focus shifts to ensuring that these systems continue to operate effectively and evolve with the organisation's needs. Regular monitoring, maintenance, user feedback, and compliance checks are integral to this phase.

Chapter 7:
Measuring AI Impact and Success

Key Performance Indicators (KPIs) for AI

Key Performance Indicators (KPIs) are essential tools for measuring the success and impact of Artificial Intelligence (AI) initiatives within an organisation. The following thoughts show how to identify and establish effective KPIs for AI projects.

Identifying Relevant KPIs

Alignment with Objectives: Ensure that KPIs are closely aligned with the specific objectives of the AI initiative. If the goal is to improve efficiency, KPIs might include metrics like process time reduction or cost savings.

Quantifiable Metrics: Choose KPIs that are quantifiable and can be measured accurately. This might include error rates, model accuracy, user engagement metrics, or revenue increases attributable to AI.

Types of AI KPIs

Performance Metrics: Measure the technical performance of AI systems, such as accuracy, speed, and reliability.

Business Impact Metrics: Assess the impact of AI on business outcomes. These could include increased sales, customer satisfaction scores, or reduced operational costs.

Operational Efficiency Metrics: Track improvements in operational processes, like reductions in manual workload, increased throughput, or enhanced resource utilisation.

Innovation and Growth Metrics: Measure the contribution of AI to new product developments, market expansions, or other growth-related activities.

Setting Benchmarks and Targets

Benchmarking: Establish benchmarks for KPIs based on industry standards, past performance, or competitive analysis. Benchmarks provide a baseline for measuring progress.

Target Setting: Set specific, achievable targets for each KPI. Targets should be challenging yet realistic, providing clear goals for the AI initiative.

Regular Monitoring and Reporting

Continuous Monitoring: Implement systems for continuous monitoring of KPIs. This allows for timely detection of issues and assessment of AI performance.

Regular Reporting: Regularly report on KPIs to stakeholders. This includes not just successes but also areas where performance is below expectations, fostering transparency and continuous improvement.

Adapting KPIs Over Time

Review and Adjust KPIs: Periodically review KPIs to ensure they remain relevant and aligned with evolving business goals and AI capabilities.

Flexibility in Metrics: Be prepared to adjust KPIs as the AI project evolves and as new insights are gained about the AI system's performance and impact.

Incorporating Qualitative Assessments

Beyond Quantitative Metrics: Include qualitative assessments to capture the broader impact of AI, such as user satisfaction, employee feedback, or changes in customer behaviour.

Effective KPIs are crucial for tracking the performance and impact of AI initiatives, providing measurable insights into how well AI aligns with and supports business objectives. Choosing the right KPIs, setting benchmarks and targets, and regular monitoring are key to understanding and maximising the value of AI investments.

Long-Term Impact of AI on Business Performance

Understanding and measuring the long-term impact of Artificial Intelligence (AI) on business performance is crucial for organisations to justify AI investments and strategically plan for future AI initiatives. It is important to know how to assess and quantify the sustained effects of AI on various aspects of business performance.

Evaluating Strategic Outcomes

Alignment with Strategic Goals: Assess how AI initiatives align with and contribute to the organisation's long-term strategic goals. This includes areas such as market growth, competitive positioning, and innovation.

Long-Term Business Transformation: Evaluate the role of AI in driving long-term business transformation, such as entering new markets, developing new business models, or reshaping customer engagement strategies.

Quantifying Financial Impact

Revenue Growth: Measure the contribution of AI to revenue growth, including new revenue streams enabled by AI and enhancements in existing revenue channels.

Cost Savings and Efficiency Gains: Quantify cost savings and efficiency gains attributable to AI, such as reductions in operational costs, improved resource utilisation, and decreased time-to-market.

Impact on Customer Experience and Satisfaction

Enhanced Customer Experience: Assess improvements in customer experience resulting from AI, such as personalised services, improved product recommendations, or faster response times.

Customer Satisfaction Metrics: Track changes in customer satisfaction metrics, including Net Promoter Score (NPS), customer retention rates, and customer feedback.

Employee Productivity and Engagement

Productivity Improvements: Evaluate the impact of AI on employee productivity, including the reduction of repetitive tasks and enabling more strategic work.

Employee Engagement and Skills Development: Assess changes in employee engagement and the development of new skills among the workforce because of AI adoption.

Innovation and Market Competitiveness

Acceleration of Innovation: Measure the contribution of AI to accelerating innovation within the organisation, including the development of new products and services.

Competitive Advantage: Evaluate how AI has enhanced the organisation's competitive advantage, such as through superior data insights, advanced customer analytics, or operational efficiencies.

Long-Term Risk Management

Mitigation of Business Risks: Assess how AI has contributed to long-term risk management, including predictive analytics for risk assessment and decision-making support.

Sustainability and Scalability: Evaluate the sustainability and scalability of AI solutions, ensuring they are adaptable to future business needs and market changes.

Assessing the long-term impact of AI on business performance requires a comprehensive view, looking beyond immediate results to understand how AI drives strategic outcomes, financial performance, customer satisfaction, employee productivity, and market competitiveness. This long-term perspective is essential for justifying AI investments and guiding future AI strategies.

Continuously Improving AI Capabilities

For organisations to stay competitive and derive ongoing value from Artificial Intelligence (AI), it is crucial to focus on continuously improving AI capabilities. The following strategies are for ensuring that AI systems evolve and remain effective over time.

Regular Evaluation and Updating of AI Models

Ongoing Model Assessment: Regularly evaluate AI models for accuracy and relevance. Monitor for any drift in data or changes in the environment that might impact model performance.

Model Updating and Retraining: Periodically update and retrain AI models with new data to keep them effective. This is particularly important in rapidly changing fields or where new data can significantly alter outcomes.

Adapting to Technological Advances

Staying Informed on AI Developments: Keep abreast of the latest developments in AI and machine learning. Evaluate how emerging technologies and techniques can enhance existing AI systems.

R&D Investment: Invest in research and development to explore new AI methodologies and tools. Consider partnerships with academic institutions or technology companies to leverage external expertise.

Feedback Loops and User Engagement

Gathering User Feedback: Actively gather feedback from users of AI systems. User insights can reveal practical improvements and enhancements that can be made.

Iterative Development Based on Feedback: Implement a process for incorporating user feedback into iterative development cycles, ensuring that AI systems are continually refined to meet user needs better.

Fostering a Culture of AI Innovation

Encouraging Experimentation: Create an organisational culture that encourages experimentation with AI. Allow teams to explore innovative uses of AI and propose fresh solutions.

Cross-Functional Collaboration: Foster collaboration between different departments and teams to generate fresh ideas and new perspectives on using AI.

Enhancing Data Management Practices

Improving Data Quality: Continuously work on improving the quality of data used for training AI models. This includes regular data cleaning, augmentation, and validation.

Expanding Data Sources: Explore new data sources that can provide additional insights and improve AI model performance. Ensure that data collection aligns with ethical standards and privacy regulations.

Skills Development and Training

Ongoing AI Education: Provide ongoing training and education opportunities for employees to keep up with AI advancements. This includes both technical training for AI teams and broader AI literacy programs for the wider workforce.

Talent Development: Focus on developing in-house AI talent, including nurturing a pipeline of young talent and providing opportunities for career progression in AI-related roles.

Continuously improving AI capabilities is a dynamic process involving regular updates to AI models, adaptation to new technologies, user feedback incorporation, fostering an innovation-friendly culture, and enhancing data and skills management. Such ongoing improvement ensures that AI systems remain effective, relevant, and aligned with the evolving needs of the organisation.

The Role of Analytics in Measuring AI Success

Analytics play a crucial role in measuring and understanding the success of Artificial Intelligence (AI) initiatives. They can be used to derive insights from AI outcomes, evaluate performance, and guide decision-making.

Utilising Advanced Analytics for AI Performance Insights

Data-Driven Insights: Leverage advanced analytics tools to process and analyse data generated by AI systems. This can reveal insights into the effectiveness, efficiency, and impact of AI initiatives.

Performance Benchmarking: Use analytics to benchmark AI performance against pre-set targets, industry standards, or historical data. This helps in objectively assessing the success of AI projects.

Identifying Patterns and Trends through Analytics

Trend Analysis: Employ analytics to identify trends and patterns in AI system outputs. Understanding these trends is key to evaluating the long-term effectiveness and adaptability of AI solutions.

Predictive Analytics: Utilise predictive analytics to forecast future AI performance and potential impacts on business processes. This can inform strategic planning and resource allocation.

Enhancing Decision-Making with AI Analytics

Data-Driven Decisions: Use insights gained from analytics to make informed decisions about AI strategies and investments. This includes decisions on scaling AI projects, refining models, or exploring new AI applications.

Feedback Loop for Improvement: Establish a feedback loop where analytics insights are continuously used to improve AI models and systems. This iterative process ensures ongoing enhancement of AI capabilities.

Measuring ROI of AI Initiatives

Quantifying Financial Impact: Use analytics to quantify the financial impact of AI initiatives, such as return on investment (ROI), cost savings, and revenue generation.

Balancing Quantitative and Qualitative Measures: Combine quantitative data analysis with qualitative assessments to gain a comprehensive view of AI's business impact.

Communicating AI Success through Data Visualisation

Visual Representation: Utilise data visualisation tools to communicate the outcomes and success of AI initiatives to stakeholders. Effective visualisations can make complex data more understandable and actionable.

Reporting and Dashboards: Develop AI performance dashboards and reports that provide regular updates to key stakeholders, highlighting key metrics, achievements, and areas for improvement.

Leveraging Analytics for Regulatory Compliance and Ethical Oversight

Compliance Monitoring: Use analytics to ensure that AI systems comply with relevant regulations and ethical standards. This includes monitoring for data privacy compliance, bias detection, and ethical use of AI.

Audit Trails: Maintain comprehensive analytics records as audit trails. This transparency is crucial for regulatory compliance and building trust among stakeholders.

Analytics are indispensable in measuring the success of AI, providing insights that guide decision-making, performance improvement, and effective communication of AI achievements. The role of analytics extends from performance measurement to strategic planning, financial assessment, and regulatory compliance.

Case Studies: Quantifying AI's Business Value

Exploring real-world case studies where AI's business value has been quantified can provide practical insights and demonstrate the tangible benefits of AI. Below is a further selection of case studies from across various industries, highlighting how organisations have successfully measured and realised the value of their AI investments.

Case Study 1: E-commerce - Enhanced Customer Targeting

Overview: An e-commerce company implemented AI for personalised customer targeting and recommendation systems.
Company: A leading global e-commerce

platform.

AI Implementation: The company implemented machine learning algorithms to analyse customer behaviour data, including past purchases, search history, and browsing patterns. The AI system used this data to personalise product recommendations for each user.

Quantifiable Outcomes: As a result, the company saw a 35% increase in sales attributed to the personalised recommendation engine. There was also a noticeable improvement in customer retention, with a 25% increase in repeat purchases within six months of implementation.

Case Study 2: Banking - AI in Fraud Detection

Overview: A banking institution employed AI for real-time fraud detection and risk assessment.
Bank: A major international banking institution.

AI Implementation: The bank deployed an AI-based fraud detection system that analysed transaction patterns in real-time to identify anomalies indicative of fraudulent activity.

Quantifiable Outcomes: The system reduced false positives by 40%, saving significant costs in fraud investigation resources. Moreover, the bank reported a 30% reduction in actual fraudulent transaction occurrences, amounting to annual savings of several million dollars.

Case Study 3: Healthcare - Predictive Analytics for Patient Care

Overview: A healthcare provider used AI for predictive analytics in patient care management. **Healthcare Provider:** A large network of hospitals and clinics.

AI Implementation: The provider used AI to analyse electronic health records, lab results, and patient histories to predict high-risk patients for chronic diseases like diabetes and heart conditions.

Quantifiable Outcomes: This led to a 20% reduction in hospital readmissions due to better preventative care and patient management. The provider also reported a 15% decrease in emergency room visits, attributing this to more effective early intervention measures.

Case Study 4: Manufacturing - AI for Predictive Maintenance

Overview: A manufacturing company implemented AI for predictive maintenance of its machinery and equipment.

Manufacturer: An industrial equipment manufacturing company.

AI Implementation: The company applied AI models to predict equipment failures by analysing sensor data, operational logs, and maintenance records.

Quantifiable Outcomes: The predictive maintenance program resulted in a 25% reduction in unplanned downtime and a 30% decrease in maintenance costs. The lifespan of equipment was extended by an average of 20%, leading to substantial capital savings.

Case Study 5: Marketing - AI-Driven Campaign Optimisation

Overview: A marketing firm utilised AI algorithms for optimising advertising campaigns and analysing consumer behaviour.

Marketing Firm: A digital marketing agency specialising in online advertising.

AI Implementation: The firm used AI to optimise ad placements and content targeting based on real-time analysis of user engagement and conversion data.

Quantifiable Outcomes: The AI-driven campaigns achieved a 50% higher click-through rate and a 35% improvement in conversion rates compared to traditional campaigns. The firm also reported a 40% increase in ROI for their advertising spend.

Lessons and Best Practices

Clear Measurement Metrics: Each case study underscores the importance of establishing clear metrics for measuring AI's impact, such as revenue growth, cost savings, efficiency improvements, and customer satisfaction.

Alignment with Business Goals: These examples highlight how AI initiatives aligned with specific business goals can lead to quantifiable and significant benefits.

Continuous Monitoring and Adaptation: The success of these AI projects was bolstered by continuous monitoring of performance and ongoing adaptations to optimise AI systems.

These case studies demonstrate how AI can create substantial business value across different industries. They provide insights into effective strategies for measuring AI's impact and showcase the diverse applications of AI in driving business success.

Chapter 8:
The Future of AI and Organisational Strategy

Emerging Trends in AI

Staying abreast of emerging trends in Artificial Intelligence (AI) is crucial for organisations looking to harness its full potential. These are the latest developments and future directions in AI technology that are shaping its application and impact across various industries.

Advancements in Machine Learning Algorithms

Self-Supervised Learning: This emerging trend involves algorithms that can learn to understand and label data without human intervention, significantly expanding AI's learning capabilities.

Explainable AI (XAI): There is a growing emphasis on making AI decisions more transparent and understandable, which is crucial for applications in sectors like healthcare and finance.

AI and Automation

Robotic Process Automation (RPA) and AI: The integration of AI with RPA is creating more intelligent and adaptable automation solutions, capable of handling complex tasks beyond rule-based processes.

Hyperautomation: This trend involves the use of advanced technologies, including AI, to automate as many business processes as possible, enhancing efficiency and decision-making.

AI in Edge Computing

Edge AI: The processing of AI algorithms on local devices, known as Edge AI, is gaining traction. It reduces latency and enhances data privacy by processing data closer to where it is being generated.

Quantum AI

Quantum Computing and AI: The intersection of quantum computing and AI holds the promise of solving complex problems much faster than classical computers, potentially revolutionising fields like drug discovery and material science.

AI for Sustainability

AI for Environmental Solutions: AI is increasingly being used to tackle environmental challenges, from climate modelling and renewable energy optimisation to wildlife conservation.

AI Ethics and Governance

Focus on Ethical AI: As AI becomes more prevalent, the focus on ethical AI is intensifying, with organisations and governments emphasising the development of AI in an ethical, transparent, and accountable manner.

AI Governance Frameworks: There is a trend towards establishing robust governance frameworks to guide the ethical development and deployment of AI.

Personalisation and AI

Personalisation at Scale: AI is enabling personalisation at an unprecedented scale, particularly in marketing, retail, and content delivery, creating more tailored and engaging user experiences.

AI in Healthcare

AI-Driven Healthcare Innovations: AI is revolutionising healthcare with trends like personalised medicine, AI in diagnostics, and robotic surgeries, offering more precise and effective treatment options.

These emerging trends in AI showcase the rapid evolution of the technology and its expanding impact on different sectors. Keeping up with these trends is essential for organisations to capitalise on AI opportunities and remain competitive.

Preparing for the Evolving AI Landscape

As the landscape of Artificial Intelligence (AI) continues to evolve rapidly, organisations must adapt and prepare for the changes and advancements in this field. We all need strategies for staying ahead in the rapidly changing AI landscape.

Staying Informed About Technological Advancements

Continuous Learning: Encourage a culture of continuous learning within the organisation. Regularly update the team on the latest AI developments through workshops, seminars, and online courses.

Industry Engagement: Stay engaged with the AI community, including industry groups, academic institutions, and technology forums, to keep abreast of latest trends and technologies.

Investing in Research and Development

In-house R&D: Invest in in-house research and development initiatives focused on AI. Explore new applications of AI that could benefit your business.

Collaborative Research: Consider collaborative projects with universities, tech startups, or research institutions to explore innovative AI applications and share knowledge.

Building a Flexible AI Strategy

Adaptable AI Roadmap: Develop an AI strategy that is adaptable and can evolve with technological advancements. Be prepared to pivot or shift focus based on new opportunities and insights.

Scalable Solutions: Focus on scalable AI solutions that can grow and adapt with your business needs and technological changes.

Fostering an Agile Organisational Culture

Agility in Decision-Making: Encourage agility in decision-making processes, allowing for quick adoption and implementation of new AI technologies.

Risk Tolerance: Cultivate a culture that tolerates calculated risks, which is essential for innovation and taking advantage of emerging AI opportunities.

Developing a Skilled Workforce

AI Skill Development: Continuously develop the AI skills of your workforce. This includes not only technical skills but also the ability to understand and leverage AI insights in decision-making.

Attracting AI Talent: Focus on attracting top AI talent by offering a stimulating work environment, opportunities for growth, and engagement in innovative projects.

Ethical and Responsible AI Adoption

Ethical AI Practices: Ensure that the adoption of new AI technologies aligns with ethical AI practices.

Regularly review and update your ethical guidelines to reflect new developments.

Regulatory Compliance: Stay updated on AI-related regulations and ensure compliance as the legal landscape evolves.

Preparing for Disruption

Anticipating Market Changes: Use AI to anticipate and prepare for market changes. This includes analysing market trends and customer behaviour to stay ahead of the competition.

Business Model Innovation: Be open to rethinking and innovating your business model as AI technologies create new opportunities and disrupt traditional industries.

Preparing for the evolving AI landscape involves staying informed, investing in R&D, building a flexible strategy, fostering an agile culture, developing skilled talent, and ensuring ethical and responsible AI adoption. These strategies will help organisations to not only adapt to the changes AI brings but also to leverage these advancements to gain a competitive edge.

Building Sustainable and Future-Proof AI Strategies

In an ever-evolving technological landscape, developing AI strategies that are sustainable and adaptable to future changes is critical. How we approach the creation of AI strategies that can withstand technological shifts and continue to deliver value over time is obviously important.

Emphasising Scalability and Adaptability

Scalable AI Solutions: Design AI strategies and solutions with scalability in mind, allowing for expansion and modification as the organisation grows and market conditions change.

Flexible Frameworks: Adopt flexible frameworks for AI implementation that can easily integrate innovative technologies and methodologies as they emerge.

Integrating AI with Broader Business Strategies

Alignment with Business Objectives: Ensure that AI initiatives align closely with the broader business strategy and objectives, reinforcing and accelerating overall business goals.

Long-Term Vision: Develop a long-term vision for AI in your organisation, considering how emerging

AI trends might influence your industry and business model.

Focusing on Sustainable AI Practices

Ethical AI Use: Incorporate sustainable and ethical AI practices, ensuring that AI solutions are developed and used responsibly, with consideration for societal and environmental impacts.

Data Governance: Establish robust data governance policies to ensure the ethical and secure use of data, which is crucial for sustainable AI practices.

Investing in Continuous Learning and Development

Ongoing Skill Development: Foster a culture of continuous learning and development, ensuring that your workforce stays current with the latest AI technologies and practices.

Research and Innovation: Encourage research and innovation within your organisation to explore new AI applications and techniques, keeping your strategies fresh and relevant.

Developing Resilient AI Systems

Risk Management: Build resilience into your AI systems by incorporating robust risk management strategies, including regular reviews of AI performance and impact.

Contingency Planning: Develop contingency plans for potential disruptions or shifts in technology, ensuring that your AI systems can adapt, or pivot as needed.

Staying Informed and Connected

Market Awareness: Maintain a keen awareness of market trends and technological advancements in AI. This includes monitoring competitor activities and industry developments.

Networking and Collaborations: Engage in networking and collaborations with other organisations, academic institutions, and AI thought leaders to share insights and best practices.

Leveraging AI for Innovation

Driving Business Innovation: Use AI not just for operational efficiency but also as a tool for driving business innovation, exploring new products, services, and market opportunities.

Customer-Centric AI Approaches: Align AI initiatives with customer needs and preferences, ensuring that your AI strategy contributes to improved customer experiences and satisfaction.

Building sustainable and future-proof AI strategies involves an approach that is scalable, flexible, and closely aligned with broader business objectives. It requires a commitment to continuous learning, ethical practices, and innovation. This ensures that AI not only addresses current needs but is also poised to adapt and evolve with future technological advancements.

The Impact of AI on Workforce and Skills Development

The rapid advancement of Artificial Intelligence (AI) is significantly impacting the workforce and the nature of skills development. AI is reshaping job roles, and the skills required for our future workforce, therefore we must have strategies for workforce transformation in the age of AI.

Changing Nature of Job Roles

Automation and Job Transformation: AI and automation are transforming traditional job roles, automating routine tasks, and creating opportunities for employees to engage in more strategic and creative work.

Emergence of New Job Categories: AI is leading to the creation of new job categories, such as AI specialists, data scientists, and AI ethics officers, which require specialised skills and knowledge.

Impact on Skills Requirements

Shift in Skill Sets: There is a shift in the skill sets required in the AI-driven workforce. Skills in data analysis, machine learning, and AI application are becoming increasingly important.

Soft Skills and AI Complementarity: Alongside technical skills, soft skills like critical thinking, problem-solving, and adaptability are becoming more crucial as they complement AI capabilities.

Strategies for Workforce Transformation

Reskilling and Upskilling Initiatives: Implement reskilling and upskilling programs to prepare the existing workforce for the evolving job landscape. This includes providing training in AI-related skills and technologies.

Continuous Learning Culture: Foster a culture of continuous learning and development, encouraging employees to stay abreast of new technologies and trends in AI.

Collaboration Between Humans and AI

Augmentation, Not Replacement: Emphasise the narrative that AI is intended to augment human capabilities, not replace them. Highlight how AI tools can assist and enhance human work.

Human-Centric AI Design: Design AI systems that are intuitive and user-friendly, enabling effective collaboration between humans and AI.

Educational System Adaptation

Curriculum Updates: Advocate for the adaptation of educational systems to include AI and data literacy, ensuring future generations are prepared for an AI-driven world.

Partnerships with Educational Institutions: Collaborate with universities and educational institutions to align courses and programs with the changing job market and skill demands.

Addressing Workforce Displacement Concerns

Transition Support: Provide support for employees whose roles are significantly impacted by AI, including career counselling, job transition services, and retraining programs.

Ethical Considerations: Address the ethical implications of AI in the workforce, ensuring that workforce transformation due to AI adoption is managed responsibly and inclusively.

The impact of AI on the workforce and skills development is profound, necessitating a proactive approach to workforce transformation. By focusing on reskilling, fostering a culture of continuous learning, and designing human-centric AI systems, organisations can effectively navigate the challenges and opportunities presented by AI in the workforce.

Global Perspectives on AI Adoption and Regulation

The adoption and regulation of Artificial Intelligence (AI) vary significantly across the globe, influenced by cultural, economic, and political factors. Here I've shown a comparative analysis of how different regions and countries are embracing and regulating AI, and the implications of these variations for the global AI landscape.

Comparative Analysis of Regional AI Adoption

North America: In the United States and Canada, there is a strong focus on innovation and commercialisation of AI, with significant investments from both private and public sectors. The regulatory approach is generally more market driven.

Europe: The European Union is characterised by its emphasis on ethical guidelines and robust data protection laws like GDPR. The EU is actively working on comprehensive AI legislation that balances innovation with citizen rights and ethical standards.

Asia: Countries like China, Japan, and South Korea are rapidly advancing in AI, each with unique approaches. China's AI development is state driven with substantial government support, while Japan and South Korea combine government initiatives with strong private sector collaboration.

Emerging Economies: Countries like India, Brazil, and South Africa are also making strides in AI adoption, focusing on AI's potential to address local challenges and improve public services, although they face hurdles like data infrastructure and investment.

Diverse Approaches to AI Governance

Regulatory Frameworks: There is significant diversity in AI regulatory frameworks. While some countries focus on fostering innovation with minimal regulation, others prioritise stringent ethical and legal standards.

International Cooperation: Differences in AI governance underscore the need for international cooperation and dialogue to develop global norms and standards for AI.

Global Implications of AI Adoption Variations

Competitiveness and Collaboration: The variations in AI adoption impact global competitiveness and influence opportunities for international collaboration in AI research and development.

Cross-Border Data Flows and AI Services: Differing regulatory environments affect cross-border data flows and the international provision of AI services, posing challenges for global AI companies.

Adapting to Regional Regulatory Landscapes

Multinational Strategy Development: Organisations operating globally need to develop AI strategies that are adaptable to different regional regulatory landscapes, respecting local laws and cultural contexts.

Ethical and Responsible AI Adoption: Despite regional differences, there is a growing global consensus on the need for ethical and responsible AI adoption. Multinational organisations should adhere to these universal principles.

Understanding the global perspectives on AI adoption and regulation is crucial for any organisation operating internationally or planning to expand its AI initiatives across borders. The diverse approaches to AI governance across different regions reflect varied priorities and can significantly impact the strategy and operations of AI projects.

Chapter 9:
Appendices

Glossary of AI Terms

This is a comprehensive list of AI-related terms, along with their definitions, to help demystify the jargon and technical language used throughout the book.

AI Glossary

AI Ethics: The branch of ethics that examines AI's moral issues and challenges, focusing on the development and implementation of AI in a manner that respects human rights and values.

AI Governance: A framework that guides the ethical and responsible development, deployment, and use of AI technologies, ensuring that AI systems are transparent, fair, and accountable.

Algorithmic Bias: Occurs when an AI system reflects implicit values or prejudices in its decision-making due to biased data inputs or flawed algorithm design.

Anomaly Detection: The identification of rare items, events, or observations which raise suspicions by differing significantly from most of the data.

Artificial Intelligence (AI): A field of computer science dedicated to creating systems capable of performing tasks that typically require human intelligence, such as visual perception, speech recognition, decision-making, and language translation.

Augmented Intelligence: A design pattern for a human-centred partnership model of people and AI working together to enhance cognitive performance, including learning, decision making, and new experiences.

Autonomous Vehicles: Vehicles equipped with AI systems that can perform the tasks of driving without human intervention by sensing their environment and navigating appropriately.

Big Data: Extremely large data sets that may be analysed computationally to reveal patterns, trends, and associations, especially relating to human behaviour and interactions.

Chatbot: An AI application designed to simulate conversation with human users, particularly over the internet, using text or voice interactions.

Cognitive Computing: A complex computing system that mimics the human brain's functioning, processing data and creating patterns to make decisions.

Computer Vision: An AI field that trains computers to interpret and understand the visual world, processing images and videos to make decisions or recommendations.

Copilot: This term is often used in the context of AI-assisted coding or development tools. An AI copilot helps programmers by suggesting code, completing lines or blocks of code, and providing information or recommendations based on the context of the development task. Microsoft have also used this name for their AI assistance.

Data Mining: The process of discovering patterns and extracting useful information from large data sets using machine learning, statistics, and database systems.

Deep Learning (DL): A branch of machine learning based on artificial neural networks with representation learning. Deep learning can learn from unstructured data like images and text.

Edge AI: AI computations performed at or near the

source of the data (e.g., on local devices, rather than in a centralised data-processing facility).

Explainable AI (XAI): AI systems that provide human-understandable insights into their decision-making process, enhancing transparency.

Facial Recognition: An AI technology capable of identifying or verifying a person from a digital image or a video frame from a video source, often used in security systems.

Foundational AI: Refers to AI systems that form the underlying basis or foundation for specific applications or further AI developments. These systems provide fundamental capabilities that can be built upon or adapted for various use cases.

General AI: Refers to the concept of a general-purpose, versatile AI system that can understand, learn, and apply its intelligence broadly and flexibly, similar to human cognitive abilities. Unlike narrow AI, which excels in specific tasks, GenAI can theoretically perform a wide range of tasks with human-like adaptability.

Generative Adversarial Network (GAN): A class of machine learning frameworks where two neural networks contest with each other to generate new, synthetic instances of data that can pass for real data.

Generative AI: A type of AI that can generate new content, including text, images, and audio, based on its training data. It uses deep learning techniques to produce outputs that can be novel and creative, such as artwork, music, or realistic human-like text.

Hallucinations: In AI, hallucinations refer to instances where an AI model generates incorrect, nonsensical, or unrelated outputs, often due to limitations in its understanding or processing of the input data.

Large Language Models (LLM): These are advanced machine learning models designed to understand, generate, and work with human language at a large scale. They are trained on vast datasets of text and are capable of tasks like translation, summarisation, and answering questions.

Machine Learning (ML): A subset of AI where machines learn to perform tasks by analysing and learning from data, rather than through explicit programming.

Machine Vision: The technology and methods used to provide imaging-based automatic inspection and analysis for applications such as automatic inspection, process control, and robot guidance.

Natural Language Generation (NLG): The use of AI to generate text similar to human-written texts, often used in chatbots and to create reports or summaries from data.

Natural Language Processing (NLP): An AI technology focused on enabling computers to understand, interpret, and respond to human language in a useful and meaningful way.

Neural Network: A computational model inspired by the human brain's structure, consisting of interconnected nodes (like neurons) that process information in layers.

Parameters: In the context of AI and machine learning, parameters are the parts of the model that are learned from the training data. They are the aspects of the model that are adjusted to make accurate predictions or decisions.

Predictive Analytics: The use of data, statistical algorithms, and machine learning techniques to identify the likelihood of future outcomes based on historical data.

Prompting: In AI, prompting refers to the act of providing an AI system, especially language models, with a text input (prompt) that guides or triggers the system to generate a specific response or output.

Quantum AI: The application of quantum computing principles and technologies to improve the capabilities and performance of AI algorithms.

Reinforcement Learning: A type of machine learning where an agent learns to make decisions by performing actions and receiving feedback from those actions.

Robotic Process Automation (RPA): Technology that automates routine and repetitive tasks typically performed by humans in business processes.

Rule Number 34: While not a specific AI term, in internet culture, Rule 34 is an adage which asserts that if something exists, there is porn of it on the internet. It's important to note that responsible and ethical AI development involves putting safeguards against AI being used to generate or promote harmful or inappropriate content.

Sentiment Analysis: An AI technique used to determine the emotional tone behind words, to gain an understanding of the attitudes, opinions, and emotions expressed in an online mention.

Supervised Learning: A type of machine learning where the model is trained on labelled data (data with known outcomes).

Transfer Learning: A machine learning method where a model developed for a task is reused as the starting point for a model on a second task, helping to improve learning efficiency and model performance.

Unsupervised Learning: A machine learning technique where the model learns from data that is not labelled and identifies patterns and relationships within the data.

List of Useful Resources for Further Reading

To further explore and understand the rapidly evolving field of Artificial Intelligence (AI), a variety of resources can be invaluable. This is a curated list of recommended AI resources, including books, websites, journals, and online courses that I rate, and which offer valuable insights and information.

Books

Artificial Intelligence: A Guide for Thinking Humans by Melanie Mitchell: Provides a critical examination of the current state of AI and its potential future.

https://amsn.to/477aB1E

Life 3.0: Being Human in the Age of Artificial

Intelligence by Max Tegmark: Explores the future of AI and its impact on the fabric of human existence.

https://amsn.to/46Ws0ah

Superintelligence: Paths, Dangers, Strategies by Nick Bostrom: Discusses the future prospects and ethical considerations of superintelligent AI systems.

https://amsn.to/3tkgcnq

Scary Smart: The Future of Artificial Intelligence and How You Can Save Our World by Mo Gawdat: Challenges readers to think critically about the trajectory of AI and their role in influencing its path.

https://amsn.to/3thU4u1

Rewired: Guide to Outcompeting in the Age of Digital and AI by McKinsey & Company: Offers insights and strategies on how businesses can leverage digital transformation and technology, including AI, to drive innovation, efficiency, and competitive advantage in the modern digital economy.

https://amsn.to/48kLYiS

Human Compatible: AI and the Problem of

Control by Stuart Russell: A thought-provoking book that explores the future of Artificial Intelligence and advocates for the development of AI systems that are inherently designed to be beneficial to and compatible with human values and interests.

https://amsn.to/48DEwQr

The Coming Wave: A.I., Power and the Twenty-First Century's Greatest Dilemma by Mustafa Suleyman: A forward-looking book that delves into the transformative impact of Artificial Intelligence on power structures and societal dynamics, posing critical questions about how AI will shape the major dilemmas of the 21st century.

https://amsn.to/472m7vj

Websites and Online Portals

AI Trends: Offers the latest news, insights, and analysis in the field of AI and machine learning.

https://www.aitrends.com/

MIT News - Artificial Intelligence: Provides cutting-edge research news and articles from one of the leading institutions in AI research.

https://news.mit.edu/topic/artificial-intelligence2

Towards Data Science: A Medium publication offering a platform for thousands of writers to share their thoughts on data science, machine learning, and AI.

https://towardsdatascience.com/

ACM Transactions on Intelligent Systems and Technology (TIST): TIST is a scholarly journal that publishes peer-reviewed research covering a broad range of topics within AI, machine learning, and intelligent systems.

https://dl.acm.org/journal/tist

Journal of Artificial Intelligence Research (JAIR): JAIR offers free access to original, high-quality research papers and articles in all areas of artificial intelligence.

https://www.jair.org/

IEEE Transactions on Pattern Analysis and Machine Intelligence (TPAMI): TPAMI is a respected journal that focuses on research in pattern analysis, machine vision, and the application of machine learning techniques.

https://www.computer.org/csdl/journal/tp

Journal of Machine Learning Research (JMLR): JMLR provides an open-access platform for the publication of new algorithms and experimental studies in the broad field of machine learning.

http://www.jmlr.org/

AI & Society: AI & Society is an international journal exploring the societal implications of AI and the impact of AI on human life and societal structures.

https://www.springer.com/journal/146

Ethics and Information Technology: This journal critically examines the ethical dimensions and the interplay between ethics, information technology, and society.

https://www.springer.com/journal/10676

Data & Society: Data & Society is a research institute focused on social, cultural, and ethical issues arising from data-centric technological development.

https://datasociety.net/

Academic Journals

Artificial Intelligence Journal (AIJ): One of the oldest and most established journals, AIJ publishes articles on a wide range of topics in AI, including theory, methods, and applications.

https://www.journals.elsevier.com/artificial-intelligence

Journal of Artificial Intelligence Research: JAIR is a high-visibility, open-access journal that disseminates significant, original research in all areas of Artificial Intelligence.

https://www.jair.org/

IEEE Transactions on Pattern Analysis and Machine Intelligence: TPAMI is a leading journal in computer vision and pattern recognition, focusing on research with applications in AI and machine learning.

https://www.computer.org/csdl/journal/tp

Journal of Machine Learning Research: JMLR provides an open-access platform for the AI community, publishing high-quality research on all aspects of machine learning.

http://www.jmlr.org/

Neural Networks: This journal covers neural network theory and applications, offering insights into learning algorithms and systems within AI.

https://www.journals.elsevier.com/neural-networks

AI Magazine: Offers accessible articles on a range of AI topics, intended for a broad readership including professionals, researchers, and students.

https://www.aaai.org/Magasine/magasine.php

International Journal of Robotics Research: IJRR publishes peer-reviewed research on all aspects of robotics, a field closely intertwined with AI, from foundational work to practical applications.

https://journals.sagepub.com/home/ijr

ACM Transactions on Intelligent Systems and Technology: TIST covers the spectrum of AI technologies and their applications, with a focus on the development of intelligent and autonomous systems.

https://dl.acm.org/journal/tist

Pattern Recognition: This journal is focused on pattern recognition, image analysis, and understanding, all crucial areas in the development of AI systems.

https://www.journals.elsevier.com/pattern-recognition

Cognitive Systems Research: The journal emphasises the integration of AI and cognitive science to create systems capable of intelligent behaviour.

https://www.journals.elsevier.com/cognitive-systems-research

Online Courses and Educational Platforms

Coursera - AI For Everyone by Andrew Ng: A non-technical course designed to help understand AI's capabilities and limitations.

https://www.coursera.org/learn/ai-for-everyone

edX - Artificial Intelligence MicroMasters Program by Columbia University: Offers a series of graduate-level courses for deep diving into AI.

https://www.edx.org/learn/artificial-intelligence/columbia-university-artificial-intelligence-ai

Udemy - AI Courses: Provides a wide range of courses catering to various aspects of AI, suitable for beginners and advanced learners.

https://www.udemy.com/topic/artificial-intelligence/

Microsoft Learn – Introduction to AI for Business Users: Offers a comprehensive AI learning and community hub where you can enhance your skills and prepare to drive AI transformation using the Microsoft Cloud.

https://learn.microsoft.com/en-us/training/paths/introduction-ai-for-business-users/

Podcasts on AI

The AI Podcast by NVIDIA: NVIDIA's AI Podcast offers engaging conversations with some of the leading minds in AI, exploring the latest breakthroughs and applications.

https://blogs.nvidia.com/ai-podcast/

Lex Fridman Podcast: Hosted by Lex Fridman, a researcher at MIT, this podcast features deep and thought-provoking discussions on AI, technology, philosophy, and science.

https://lexfridman.com/podcast/

AI in Business: This podcast is tailored for business leaders, exploring the real-world applications of AI in various industries and the practical aspects of AI deployment in companies.

https://emerj.com/ai-in-business-podcast/

Eye on AI: This podcast delves into the latest research and trends in AI, with interviews featuring experts, practitioners, and researchers in the field.

https://www.eye-on.ai/

Practical AI: Machine Learning & Data Science: This is a podcast that makes artificial intelligence practical, productive, and accessible to everyone, breaking down complex topics into understandable discussions.

https://changelog.com/practicalai

Video Channels on AI

Two Minute Papers: Dr Károly Zsolnai-Fehér hosts this YouTube channel, which provides easy-to-understand summaries of the latest and most exciting research papers in AI and computer science.

https://www.youtube.com/user/keeroys

Sentdex: This channel offers programming tutorials and practical demonstrations on how to implement machine learning, data analysis, and AI in various projects.

https://www.youtube.com/user/sentdex

DeepMind: The official YouTube channel for DeepMind, where they share insights into their groundbreaking research and advancements in AI.

https://www.youtube.com/user/deepmind

Arxiv Insights: Xander Steenbrugge shares his insights on the latest AI research, exploring complex topics in machine learning with clear visualisations and explanations.

https://www.youtube.com/channel/UCNIkB2IeJ-6AmSv7bQ1oBYg

MITCSAIL: The official channel for MIT's Computer Science & Artificial Intelligence Lab (CSAIL) showcases lectures, research, and advancements from one of the world's top AI research institutions.

https://www.youtube.com/user/MITCSAIL

Professional Organisations and Networks

These organisations play a crucial role in the development and dissemination of AI knowledge and practices, offering professionals opportunities for networking, education, and collaboration on a global scale.

AAAI - Association for the Advancement of Artificial Intelligence: An international non-profit scientific society devoted to promoting research in, and responsible use of, artificial intelligence.

https://www.aaai.org/

IEEE - Institute of Electrical and Electronics Engineers – CIS - Computational Intelligence

Society: IEEE CIS is a professional body dedicated to the study of computational intelligence, fostering the development and application of AI and machine learning technologies.

https://cis.ieee.org/

IAAIL International Association for Artificial Intelligence and Law: IAAIL is an organisation that promotes research and development in the field of AI with respect to the law, including applications in legal reasoning, knowledge management, and more.

http://www.iaail.org/

The Alan Turing Institute: The UK's national institute for data science and artificial intelligence, named after the pioneering British computer scientist Alan Turing, which focuses on advancing the world-changing potential of AI and data science.

https://www.turing.ac.uk/

British Computer Society - Specialist Group on Artificial Intelligence: A part of the BCS, the SGAI is dedicated to those interested in AI and its applications, promoting the understanding and responsible use of AI among practitioners and researchers in the UK.

https://www.bcs.org/membership/member-communities/specialist-group-on-artificial-intelligence-sgai/

AI Forum New Zealand: A network that brings together professionals, researchers, and industry stakeholders in New Zealand to help enable the country to benefit from AI advancements.

https://aiforum.org.ns/

EurAI - European Association for Artificial Intelligence: Formerly known as ECCAI, EurAI is a representative body for the European Artificial Intelligence community, aiming to promote AI research and development across Europe.

https://www.eurai.org/

AI & Society: A global network of professionals and researchers dedicated to examining the impact of AI on society and individuals and ensuring that AI develops in a manner that benefits humanity.

https://link.springer.com/journal/146

WAI - Women in AI: A non-profit global network of female experts and professionals in the field of AI aiming to close the gender gap and encourage female participation in AI.

https://www.womeninai.co/

International Machine Learning Society: IMLS is an organisation dedicated to the advancement of machine learning, which is intrinsically linked to AI. It is known for organising the International Conference on Machine Learning (ICML).

https://www.machinelearning.org/

AI Thought Leaders and Influencers

Staying connected with the thoughts and insights of leading figures in the field of Artificial Intelligence (AI) can provide valuable perspectives on current trends, future directions, and ethical considerations. This list shows some of the prominent AI thought leaders and influencers who I look to and whose work and opinions significantly shape the AI landscape.

Key AI Thought Leaders and Influencers

Demis Hassabis: Co-founder and CEO of DeepMind, a pioneering AI company known for developing AlphaGo. His work focuses on neural networks and deep learning.

Fei-Fei Li: A professor at Stanford University and co-director of the Stanford Human-Centred AI Institute. She is known for her work in computer vision and cognitive neuroscience.

Andrew Ng: Co-founder of Google Brain, former Chief Scientist at Baidu, and a professor at Stanford University. He is a prominent figure in machine learning and the co-founder of Coursera.

Yann LeCun: Vice President and Chief AI Scientist at Facebook and a professor at New York University. He is known for his work on convolutional neural networks and deep learning.

Geoffrey Hinton: A pioneer in the field of neural networks and deep learning, he is a professor at the University of Toronto and works with Google Brain.

Kate Crawford: A leading researcher and author focusing on the social implications of AI, data politics, and ethics in technology.

Timnit Gebru: A computer scientist known for her research on algorithmic bias and ethical AI. She is an advocate for diversity in technology.

Max Tegmark: A physicist and AI researcher at MIT, known for his advocacy in AI safety and ethical AI development.

Stuart Russell: A professor at the University of California, Berkeley, and author of the textbook "Artificial Intelligence: A Modern Approach." He is known for his research on AI and its long-term future.

Anima Anandkumar: A professor at Caltech and a director of machine learning research at NVIDIA. Her work focuses on machine learning, AI, and tensor algorithms.

Keeping up with the insights and research of these AI thought leaders can be incredibly beneficial for anyone interested in understanding the diverse and rapidly evolving field of AI. Their contributions cover a wide range of topics from technical advancements to ethical and social implications of AI (and obviously you can always follow yours truly too!).

AI Strategy Templates and Checklists

Developing a comprehensive AI strategy requires careful planning and consideration of a range of factors. Here are some templates and checklists that organisations can use as a starting point to develop and refine their AI strategies.

These serve as a guide for organisations to develop and execute an AI strategy effectively. They are designed to be customisable to fit the specific needs and contexts of different organisations.

AI Strategy Template - 1

- **Executive Summary:**
  - Brief overview of the AI strategy goals and objectives.
  - High-level description of the AI initiatives.
- **Current State Analysis:**
  - Assessment of current AI capabilities and technologies in use.
  - Analysis of data readiness and infrastructure.
- **Vision and Objectives:**
  - Long-term vision for AI in the organisation.
  - Specific AI objectives aligned with business goals.
- **Use Case Identification:**
  - Identification of potential AI use cases.
  - Prioritisation based on impact, feasibility, and strategic alignment.

- **Technology and Data Strategy:**
  - Selection of AI technologies and tools.
  - Data governance and management plan.
- **Implementation Plan:**
  - Roadmap for AI implementation including timelines and milestones.
  - Resource allocation (budget, personnel, technology).
- **Risk Management and Ethical Considerations:**
  - Identification of potential risks and mitigation strategies.
  - Ethical guidelines and compliance considerations.
- **Performance Metrics and KPIs:**
  - Key Performance Indicators (KPIs) to measure AI success.
  - Monitoring and evaluation plan.
- **Change Management and Training:**
  - Plan for managing organisational change.
  - Training and development programs for staff.
- **Futureproofing and Scalability:**
  - Strategies for ensuring the long-term sustainability and scalability of AI initiatives.
  - Adaptation plan for future AI advancements.

AI Strategy Checklist - 2

- [ ] **Define Clear AI Goals and Objectives:** Ensure your AI objectives are specific, measurable, achievable, relevant, and time-bound (SMART).
- [ ] **Conduct a Thorough Current State Assessment:** Understand existing capabilities, infrastructure, and gaps.
- [ ] **Prioritise Use Cases:** Focus on use cases with the highest potential impact and alignment with strategic goals.
- [ ] **Ensure Robust Data Management:** Prioritise data quality, accessibility, and privacy.
- [ ] **Select the Right Technology and Partners:** Choose appropriate AI technologies and consider potential partnerships for expertise and resources.

- ☐ **Develop a Comprehensive Implementation Plan:** Outline clear steps, allocate resources, and set realistic timelines.
- ☐ **Address Risks and Ethical Considerations:** Identify risks and develop mitigation strategies. Embed ethical considerations into your AI strategy.
- ☐ **Establish KPIs and Monitoring Mechanisms:** Define how success will be measured and monitored.
- ☐ **Plan for Organisational Change and Workforce Development:** Prepare the organisation and its workforce for AI adoption.
- ☐ **Stay Agile and Adaptable:** Build flexibility into your strategy to adapt to new developments and insights.

Questions for your top team

It is important that any AI transformation needs to be driven by the top team in an organisation. These six questions are designed to ensure that the board comprehensively evaluates the organisation's approach to integrating technology (AI or otherwise), in alignment with its broader business strategy and goals. They encompass key aspects of strategic planning and execution in the context of technological integration, particularly AI.

1. **Vision and Technology's Role:** Does everyone understand the company's vision and how technology, especially AI, will help achieve it? This ensures alignment of

technology with the overall business vision, a fundamental aspect of strategic planning.

2. **Business Focus Areas:** Are we focusing on the right business areas that are most likely to deliver significant, feasible value? This focuses on prioritising areas that yield the most value, ensuring resources are allocated effectively and feasibly.

3. **Benefits and Investments:** Do we have a clear understanding of the expected benefits of our technology initiatives and the investments they will require? This addresses the need for a clear understanding of the return on investment, which is crucial for informed decision-making and resource allocation.

4. **Resource Alignment for Impact:** Are our resources strategically aligned with a few key areas that have the potential to create substantial impact? This emphasises the importance of targeted efforts and resource optimisation for maximum impact, rather than diffused or scattered approaches.

5. **Building Digital Capabilities:** Are we aware of the new digital capabilities required and committed to investing in their

development? This recognises the importance of future-proofing the organisation by developing necessary digital competencies, a key for long-term competitiveness.

6. **Roles and Responsibilities:** How effectively can we define and communicate our roles, and those of our teams, in executing our digital strategy? Finally, this highlights the need for clear communication and understanding of roles in strategy implementation, crucial for accountability and effective execution.

These questions are structured to prompt a thorough and critical examination of how technology, particularly AI, is integrated into the broader business strategy. They encourage a focus on alignment, feasibility, value generation, and clear execution roles, all of which are essential for successful digital transformation initiatives.

Frequently Asked Questions about AI

These are the most frequently asked questions (FAQs) that I receive when delivering talks and strategic masterclasses about AI.

What is Artificial Intelligence (AI)?

AI is a branch of computer science that aims to create systems capable of performing tasks that would typically require human intelligence. This includes learning, problem-solving, perception, and language understanding.

How does Machine Learning (ML) differ from AI?

ML is a subset of AI focused on algorithms that learn

from data and make predictions or decisions. AI is a broader concept that includes ML but also encompasses other aspects like reasoning and natural language processing.

What is Deep Learning?

Deep Learning is a type of machine learning involving neural networks with many layers. It is particularly effective for processing substantial amounts of unstructured data like images and natural language.

Can AI surpass human intelligence?

Currently, AI excels in specific, narrow tasks but lacks the general intelligence and consciousness of humans. Whether it can surpass human intelligence is a subject of debate and speculation.

What are some common applications of AI?

AI applications include voice assistants, image recognition, autonomous vehicles, personalised recommendations, healthcare diagnostics, and chatbots, among others.

Is AI a threat to jobs?

AI is likely to transform many jobs and industries. While it may automate certain tasks, it also creates opportunities for new roles and industries, emphasising the importance of skills adaptation and training. As a rule, my take is that you won't lose your job to AI, but you might lose it to someone else who is using AI.

How does AI learn?

AI learns through algorithms that process and analyse data. In machine learning, AI learns patterns from data, improving its performance with more data and experience.

What are the ethical concerns with AI?

Ethical concerns include privacy issues, bias and fairness, transparency, job displacement, and the potential misuse of AI technology.

Can AI make decisions without human input?

Some AI systems can make certain decisions without direct human input, particularly in well-defined, narrow tasks. However, human oversight is crucial, especially in critical applications.

What is the future of AI?

The future of AI includes more advanced and integrated applications in various fields, increased focus on ethical and responsible AI, and continued research into making AI systems more efficient, fair, and transparent.

What is Natural Language Processing (NLP)?

NLP is a field of AI that focuses on enabling machines to understand, interpret, and respond to human language, both written and spoken.

How does AI impact healthcare?

In healthcare, AI is used for tasks like analysing medical images, predicting disease outbreaks, personalising treatment plans, and assisting in surgeries, potentially leading to improved patient outcomes.

What are neural networks?

Neural networks are a set of algorithms, modelled loosely after the human brain, designed to recognise patterns, and interpret sensory data through machine perception, labelling, and clustering raw input.

Is AI capable of creativity?

AI can generate novel content, like art or music, based on patterns it has learned. However, its 'creativity' is derived from data inputs and algorithms and lacks the conscious experience and emotional depth of human creativity.

What is AI bias, and how can it be prevented?

AI bias occurs when an AI system reflects biases present in its training data or algorithms. Preventing AI bias involves using diverse and representative training datasets, regularly testing AI systems for bias, and incorporating ethical guidelines.

How is AI used in business?

Businesses use AI for various purposes, including customer service automation, predictive analytics, personalisation of services, supply chain optimisation, and enhancing decision-making processes.

Can AI understand human emotions?

AI systems can recognise and interpret human emotions to a certain extent, usually through analysing speech patterns, facial expressions, or text. However, AI does not 'understand' emotions in the human sense.

What is the role of data in AI?

Data is crucial in AI; it is the foundation upon which AI models are trained and refined. The quality, quantity, and diversity of data significantly impact the performance and accuracy of AI systems.

Are AI systems transparent in their decisions?

AI transparency is a challenge, especially in complex models like deep learning. Efforts in Explainable AI (XAI) aim to make AI decision-making processes more transparent and understandable.

How does AI affect privacy?

AI can impact privacy through its ability to analyse copious amounts of personal data, raising concerns about data protection, consent, and how data is used and shared.

This is one of those lists that will constantly evolve, but each of these questions about AI are useful, hopefully providing you an increased understanding of the field.

Chapter 10: Conclusion

Summarising Key Takeaways

As we reach the conclusion of "Harnessing AI," it is evident that the AI revolution is not just a fleeting trend but a transformative force reshaping our world. This last section reflects on the key insights gained throughout the book and looks forward to how organisations and individuals can embrace and thrive in this era of AI.

Reflection on the AI Journey

The Evolution of AI: We have seen how AI has evolved from theoretical concepts to practical applications impacting every sector, driven by advancements in computing power, data availability, and algorithmic innovations.

AI's Diverse Applications: From improving healthcare outcomes to optimising business processes and enhancing customer experiences, AI's applications are vast and growing.

The Future of AI and Its Implications

Continued Advancements: AI will continue to advance, bringing more sophisticated capabilities. This will open new opportunities and pose fresh challenges.

Impact on Society and Work: AI's impact on society and the workforce will be profound. While it presents opportunities for growth and innovation, it also necessitates careful consideration of ethical, social, and economic implications.

Strategies for AI Adoption and Implementation

Adopting a Strategic Approach: Successful AI adoption requires a strategic approach, aligning AI initiatives with business objectives, focusing on data quality, ensuring ethical practices, and investing in talent and training.

Leveraging AI for Competitive Advantage: Organisations that effectively leverage AI can gain significant competitive advantages, from improved efficiencies to novel products and services.

Ethical Considerations and Responsible AI

Ethical AI Frameworks: Developing and adhering to ethical AI frameworks is crucial to ensure that AI benefits society and does not perpetuate biases or inequalities.

Governance and Regulation: As AI becomes more integral to our lives, appropriate governance and regulation will be essential to manage its societal impacts and ensure responsible use.

Preparing for the AI-Driven Future

Embracing Change: Embracing the changes brought about by AI is essential. This includes being open to new ways of working, continuous learning, and adapting to evolving job roles.

Fostering a Culture of Innovation: Cultivating a culture that embraces innovation and experimentation will be key to harnessing the potential of AI.

The Journey Ahead

Ongoing Learning and Adaptation: The journey with AI is one of ongoing learning and adaptation. Staying informed and agile will be crucial for individuals and organisations alike.

Collaborative Efforts: Collaboration between industries, academia, and governments will play a pivotal role in advancing AI technologies and addressing challenges.

I have written "Harnessing AI" to underscore the transformative power of AI and the importance of approaching it with strategy, responsibility, and a forward-looking mindset.

As we step into an AI-augmented future, the possibilities and challenges will be significant, but with careful navigation, the potential benefits for humanity and society are immense.

Future Directions in AI Research and Development

Looking beyond the current state of Artificial Intelligence (AI), it is important to consider the future directions in AI research and development, and to explore the potential advancements, emerging fields, and challenges that lie ahead in the journey of AI.

Advancements in Core AI Technologies

Improved Machine Learning Models: Continued improvement in machine learning models, including more efficient, accurate, and explainable models.

Quantum Computing in AI: Integration of quantum computing with AI, potentially revolutionising problem-solving capabilities in fields like drug discovery and climate modelling.

AI in Unexplored Domains

Expansion into New Sectors: Exploring AI applications in previously untapped sectors such as deep-sea exploration, space technology, and advanced materials research.

AI for Social Good: Increased focus on harnessing AI for addressing global challenges like poverty, education, and healthcare disparities.

Human-AI Collaboration

Augmented Intelligence: Further development of augmented intelligence, where AI enhances human decision-making and creativity, rather than replacing human input.

Ethical Human-AI Interaction: Research into ethical frameworks and models for human-AI interaction, ensuring AI systems complement and enhance human abilities responsibly.

Interdisciplinary AI Research

Cross-disciplinary Approaches: Combining AI with other fields like neuroscience, psychology, and sociology to create more sophisticated and intuitive AI systems.

AI and Environmental Science: Leveraging AI in environmental science for more accurate climate modelling, biodiversity conservation, and sustainable resource management.

Challenges and Ethical Considerations

Addressing AI Bias: Ongoing efforts to address and mitigate bias in AI systems, ensuring fairness and equality in AI-driven decisions.

AI Safety and Security: Research into AI safety and security, focusing on preventing unintended consequences of AI systems and protecting against malicious uses of AI.

AI Governance and Policy Development

Global AI Governance: Development of global governance frameworks for AI, balancing innovation with ethical, legal, and societal considerations.

Regulatory Responses to AI Advancements: Adapting and evolving regulatory responses to keep pace with AI advancements, ensuring responsible development and deployment of AI technologies.

Next-Generation AI Education and Training

AI Literacy: Fostering AI literacy at all levels of education, preparing future generations for an AI-integrated world.

Training for Emerging AI Careers: Developing educational and training programs for emerging AI-related careers, focusing on both technical and ethical aspects of AI.

The future of AI research and development promises not only technological advancements but also new opportunities and challenges at the intersection of AI and various aspects of human life. Staying ahead in this rapidly evolving field will require continuous learning, ethical consideration, and proactive adaptation to emerging trends and developments.

Final Thoughts and Encouragement for AI Adoption

In these final pages of "Harnessing AI," I want to reflect on the journey through the dynamic and evolving world of Artificial Intelligence (AI). This section is designed to leave you with thoughtful encouragement for AI adoption and insights into navigating the future of AI.

Acknowledging AI's Transformative Potential

Recognising AI's Impact: Embrace the understanding that AI is more than a technological innovation; it is a transformative force reshaping industries, societies, and the global economy.

Potential for Positive Change: Recognise AI's potential to drive positive changes, such as enhancing efficiency, fostering innovation, and solving complex global challenges.

Encouragement for AI Adoption

Start Small and Scale Up: Begin your AI journey with small, manageable projects. As confidence and understanding grow, gradually scale up your AI initiatives.
Emphasise Continuous Learning: AI is a field of constant evolution. Encourage a culture of continuous learning and curiosity within your organisation.

Balancing Innovation with Responsibility

Responsible AI Use: As you explore AI's possibilities, always consider the ethical implications of your AI applications. Responsible AI use is crucial for long-term success and societal acceptance.

Inclusive AI Development: Strive for AI development that is inclusive and considerate of diverse perspectives. This approach helps in creating AI solutions that are fair, unbiased, and beneficial to a broader population.

Looking Towards a Collaborative Future

Embrace Collaboration: The future of AI is not just in competition but also in collaboration. Engaging with other organisations, academia, and industry consortia can lead to shared learnings and advancements.

Public and Private Sector Partnerships: Encourage partnerships between the public and private sectors to foster AI innovation that aligns with societal needs and ethical standards.

Preparing for an AI-Augmented Future

Adaptability and Flexibility: The future is AI-augmented. Prepare your organisation to be adaptable and flexible, integrating AI into various processes while staying agile to changes in the AI landscape.

Investing in People: Beyond technology, invest in people. Equip your workforce with the skills and knowledge needed to work alongside AI, ensuring they are empowered rather than replaced.

A Journey of Discovery: Embracing AI is a journey of discovery, filled with challenges and opportunities. Approach it with an open mind, a commitment to ethical principles, and a willingness to learn and adapt.

A Vision for the Future: Envision a future where AI enhances human capabilities, drives sustainable growth, and creates new possibilities. Your journey with AI has the potential to shape not just the future of your organisation but also contribute to the broader narrative of technology and humanity.

Remember that AI adoption is a journey marked by continuous learning and adaptation. It offers immense potential, but it also requires thoughtful consideration and responsible action. Embrace the AI revolution with optimism, preparedness, and a commitment to ethical principles.

The Call to Action

We stand at a pivotal moment in the evolution of Artificial Intelligence (AI). This final section serves as a call to action for individuals, organisations, and societies at large, urging an active and thoughtful engagement with AI.

Embrace AI as a Catalyst for Change

Acknowledge the Potential: Recognise AI's potential to revolutionise industries, enhance human capabilities, and solve complex global issues.

Embrace Change: Welcome the changes brought by AI. View them as opportunities for growth, innovation, and progress, both at an individual and organisational level.

Engage in Lifelong Learning and Adaptation

Continuous Learning: Commit to lifelong learning. Stay informed about the latest developments in AI to understand its evolving capabilities and implications.
Adapt Skills: Adapt your skillset to complement AI. Focus on areas where human skills excel, such as creativity, empathy, and complex problem-solving.

Advocate for Ethical AI Development

Champion Ethical Practices: Advocate for the development and use of AI that is ethical, transparent, and fair. Promote practices that prevent biases and protect privacy and security.

Participate in Policy Making: Engage in policy and regulatory discussions to ensure that AI develops in a manner that benefits society and respects human dignity.

Foster Collaboration and Inclusive Dialogue

Collaborate Across Borders: Encourage collaboration across industries, disciplines, and countries. Diverse perspectives and collective wisdom are key to harnessing AI's full potential.
Inclusive Dialogue: Participate in inclusive dialogues about AI's impact on society. Ensure that

voices from different sectors, including marginalised communities, are heard, and considered.

Implement AI Responsibly in Business and Society

Responsible Implementation: In business, implement AI in ways that improve efficiency, enhance customer experiences, and create value while being mindful of its impact on employees and society.
Social Responsibility: Use AI as a tool for social good. Address societal challenges such as healthcare, education, and environmental sustainability through AI-driven solutions.

Conclusion: A Call to Lead and Innovate

Lead the Way: Be a leader in the AI revolution. Whether you are a business leader, a policymaker, an educator, or a student, you have a role to play in shaping the future of AI.

Innovate for a Better Future: Utilise AI not just for economic gain, but as a means to innovate for a better and more sustainable future for all.

This call to action is an invitation to be at the forefront of the AI revolution. It is an encouragement to embrace AI with responsibility, foresight, and an unwavering commitment to the betterment of society. The journey of AI is one of discovery, challenge, and immense potential. How we navigate this journey will define not only the future of technology but also the future of humanity itself. Let us step forward with optimism, responsibility, and a vision for a world enhanced, not overridden, by AI.

About the Author

Rob May is a thought-leader, an award-winning TEDx and international keynote speaker. He is the UK Ambassador for Cybersecurity with the IoD. Rob is the Founder and Executive Chairman of ramsac – the secure choice™, and he sits on several industry and academic advisory boards.

Rob is a Leadership Fellow at Windsor Castle, a Fellow of The IoD, Fellow of The RSA and a Fellow at BSDC where he is also the Patron for Employability, and he has The Freedom of The City of London.

Rob has been at the forefront of the technology industry for the last 35 years and his talks, books and academic sessions reflect this experience.

Harnessing AI

Printed in Great Britain
by Amazon